Hispanic
Stars
Rising

VOLUME II

THE NEW FACE OF POWER

Hispanic Stars Rising Vol. II

This book is a compilation of stories from numerous people who have each contributed a chapter and is designed to provide inspiration to our readers.

It is sold with the understanding that the publisher and the individual authors are not engaged in the rendering of psychological, legal, accounting or other professional advice. The content and views in each chapter are the sole expression and opinion of its author and not necessarily the views of Fig Factor Media, LLC.

For more information, contact:

We Are All Human | www.weareallhuman.org
Hispanic Star | www.hispanicstar.org
Fig Factor Media, LLC | www.figfactormedia.com

Cover Design & Layout by LDG Juan Manuel Serna Rosales
Printed in the United States of America

ISBN: 978-1-952779-20-6
Library of Congress Control Number: 2021919357

TO MY MOM. I AM WHO I AM
BECAUSE OF YOU, THANK YOU
FOR ALL THE LIFE LESSONS.
TO MY CHILDREN AND MY
HUSBAND. TO MY FAMILY. YOUR
SUPPORT AND STRENGTH MEAN
THE WORLD.
TO THE HISPANIC COMMUNITY.
WE'VE NEVER BEEN SO
READY AND WE'RE ABOUT TO
BREAKTHROUGH!

Table of Contents

ACKNOWLEDGEMENTS

After such a hard year, here are the stories of Hispanic heroes who continued to represent the Hispanic community through all walks of life and accomplishments.

I am grateful to all the people who shared their stories in Hispanic Stars Rising Volume II—the ups, the downs, the way they created change in their own lives and beyond. Thank you.

I want to thank the We Are All Human team for their efforts on this book and everything they do to unify our community and change the perception of it once and for all. I know the work we are doing is monumental, but the change we will make is historic.

In a year where COVID hit our Hispanic community faster and harder than other groups, I am mindful and thankful that so much of what sustained our lives came from the selfless day-to-day heroics of Hispanic essential workers. Their stories alone could fill a volume, and that is a story that still needs to be told.

In my own life, as with so many—too many—other families, COVID hit us personally with the loss of my mother.

I know that I am who I am because of her. My mother was passionate about everything she did. She was tenacious. Ambitious. Focused. Imaginative. She taught me that it was okay to be afraid sometimes, but that I should not let that fear overwhelm or paralyze. She helped me understand that while change can be scary, it's necessary to keep rising above your fear, breaking down barriers, changing perceptions. All the lessons she taught me helped me find my purpose and led me to founding We Are All Human. The best way to thank my mother is to live her values every day.

A special thank you goes to my husband, Richard, and my children, Joshua and Tamara. They surround me with their love and support, which makes all things possible.

And I am, of course, ever grateful to our big, beautiful, diverse, Hispanic community that is busy writing the next chapter of the American Dream.

FOREWORD

BY CLAUDIA ROMO EDELMAN

Last year we published our first volume of Hispanic Stars Rising. And though our hearts told us we had created something special, we were still gratified by the response we had from people all over the country. Our readers found it uplifting and inspiring to read stories of Hispanic women and men who are rising above. Stories of people who sounded familiar though they didn't know them. Stories that were as much a roadmap as a journey traveled. As it is often said, you have to see what you can be.

This year, we go to press as the new Census Data is rolled out. We are still learning from the findings, but one message is abundantly clear in the 2020 Census: The United States is more diverse and more multi-racial than ever before. That trend is accelerating, and it is powered by Hispanics.

In the past ten years, the Hispanic population grew by 23%. To give that some context, that's slightly more than half of the total population growth in the past ten years. If you zoom in on the statistics for young people, Hispanic children account for more than 25% growth—way more than any other group. Yet we do not always feel the strength of our numbers.

The economic power of Hispanics is also formidable, but not often discussed. The buying power of Hispanics is $2.6 trillion dollars. Our combined GDP would rank us as the eighth-largest in the world. Hispanics represent 40% of workforce growth and an astounding 74% of new workers in the United States are Hispanic. We are buying more homes. Starting more businesses. Paying over $200 billion in taxes and half of that amount again into Social Security. The numbers tell that story. Yet we are not really feeling our collective strength.

There is still a disconnect between our reality and perception. We haven't completely and successfully told our own story. Controlled our own narrative. There are others who diminish and disparage us. And we have struggled not only to act as a unified group but even to see ourselves as unified group with shared interests, dreams, and power.

The numbers also don't reveal the obstacles many Hispanics still continue to face—in education, healthcare and as they build businesses and careers. We lack real representation in so many sectors. We have few seats on corporate boards or in the C-suites and not enough Hispanics in Congress. In the world of TV and movies, we are barely seen in front of the camera, and there are not a great many of us behind the camera either. Hispanics are the fastest-growing population in the military but are still not reaching the upper ranks. And on and on.

If you aren't seen, you aren't heard, which makes it difficult, if not impossible, to be valued. Representation is the first step, but it must lead to inclusion and then equity.

But let's go back to the statistics because there are lessons there. They show us the combined contributions that Hispanics are making, but they lack the faces, the stories, the compelling narrative of real people who are making their mark, making a difference, making progress in concrete ways.

Our first volume of Hispanic Stars, then, filled a real need—the need to tell our story properly, through the journeys of some exceptional, extraordinary Hispanic women and men. For as long as this nation has existed, Hispanics have been part of the American story. The more we share our experience with each other, the more we learn, the greater confidence we build, the more we move ahead. The more we show who we are and what we do, we not only help to change the way we see ourselves, but how others see us, talk about us, and cover us in the media. It has a ripple effect.

There is also a second wish here, and that is that we come together as one community. Yes, the Hispanic community is enormously diverse. And so are the people who make up this volume. But we share many values in common—We are hardworking and ambitious. We love family and home. We know how to persist and push past obstacles. We know the pride of accomplishment and feel the upward lift that comes from the hard work of those who broke barriers. Our differences truly enrich us. But our similarities empower us—or will if we choose to unite around them.

It is our hope that you savor each story. Learn from them. Share them. Reach out to the people who make up these pages. In your own life, remember to help those you can. Be a mentor. A role model. A leader. We are powering the progress of the United States, and we will find our seats at the table. But we will do it faster and better together. There are Hispanic stars rising everywhere. Meet some of them on these pages. This is our time!

Claudia Romo Edelman

PREFACE

BY IVAN "PUDGE" RODRIGUEZ

There is something very special about being Latino. We believe in family and friends. In our community. We are willing to work hard for our dreams. We don't give up. And we don't give up on others. Being Latino means being passionate, proud, and persistent. We are all stars. And there are so many stories.

My story began in Vega Baja, Puerto Rico. My mother taught elementary school and my father was an electrician. My dream to be a baseball player began on empty fields, where we played by batting a ball made of rolled-up tape with a stick. And like so many Latino athletes, I learned my skills and position from my father, who taught me how to be a catcher. I practiced and practiced in Little League games. I was signed by the Texas Rangers when I was 16 and played baseball in the Major Leagues for 21 years.

Like all my childhood friends, we idolized the Puerto Rican baseball star, Roberto Clemente. He died the year I was born, but he lived large in my parents' lives, and I grew up having him as a role model both on and off the field. That is also very Hispanic — looking up to the people who came before us, who broke down barriers, who paved the path for us. And then taking the baton, running with it, and passing it on to the next generation.

Baseball is America's national pastime. It is also 40% Latino. That is not only players, but all the staff and coaches that make the game possible. That kind of representation, not to mention the love from all the Hispanic fans, gave me the support I needed to succeed.

This past year, Hispanic essential workers were Stars, putting to good use the dedication, strength and hard work that is at the heart of our culture. In the hardest of times, Hispanics showed up every day, because that's what we do.

There are Hispanic Stars everywhere. In businesses large and small. As artists, actors, and musicians. Teachers. Scientists and engineers. Journalists. Politicians. just Every job you can imagine. The truth is that stars aren't born — they are the result of our big dreams and our big hearts. They come from working hard and never losing sight of our goals. But also, from never losing sight of our heritage, our culture, our values.

In this book, you will meet 99 Hispanic Stars. Their stories are all different, but every one of them inspired me. This is what I take away: Our Hispanic Stars are dreaming large and working hard. Staying positive and close to the community. Every Star who shines lights the way forward to someone else. So, be the person you want to be and make sure you also reach out to someone else and help them, too. Together, we are already making a difference, not just to our community, but to the United States and the world. Keep the passion alive.

Muchas gracias y Dios los bendiga,

Iván Pudge Rodríguez

THAT TIME I WAS FIRED

MIGUEL ALEMANY

"I simply started to understand how I could communicate and influence using the best of two different cultures."

When I first began in my career, I never thought of myself as someone who could inspire change. I worked hard, kept my head down, and never challenged authority. It had always worked for me, up until I was hired as one of the first Hispanic engineers of a large, multinational corporation in 1979. Although I didn't realize it at the time, I was very much a minority among my colleagues and hid my extensive knowledge and expertise instead of letting it shine through.

After a year of employment, it was time for my Annual Performance Review. My boss's boss came to my office to deliver the news: The management team had done their evaluations, and my rating was not good. On a scale from 1-100 (100 being the best), I had been given a 5. I was shocked.

I had been putting in long hours and completing tasks as

requested. In my mind, I was an exemplary employee. This just did not make sense to me. When I pushed back with dismay, my boss's boss said I was meek. I was executing directives, but without any initiative.

"Simply put," he said, "you are not a good fit for the company. We are going to have to let you go." Confused, I stammered, "But I like this job. I am not 'going' anywhere."

This man just shrugged and walked out. He didn't know what to do. For the next week, I continued to show up at the office. No one spoke to me or gave me any work assignments.

Finally, a senior leader was notified of my presence. I was summoned to his office. Now he was the one confused. "Didn't we fire you two weeks ago?" he inquired. "I think that was a mistake," I said. This leader sighed and said, "Miguel, it was not a mistake. You do what you are told, this is true. But this is also the problem. If I wanted someone who does exactly what I told them to do, I would've hired a high school student. But I hired an engineer. And we pay engineers to THINK. We pay them to problem solve. We pay them to be creative."

And it was then that I realized something: The very values that he was espousing and expecting in the workplace were in direct contradiction with the values I had been nurturing and perfecting in my life as a Hispanic. I had been instructed to respect authority, not challenge it. I had been told to be humble, not assertive. I had been raised to be loyal, not inquisitive.

With this new realization, I asked for another chance and was ultimately given one. I spent the next year changing some of my intuitive behaviors. I never compromised who I was, but I learned how to adapt and advocate for myself as an engineer *and* as a Hispanic. Five years later, the man who originally fired me was reporting to me. It is critical to note that I didn't become more intelligent; my degree didn't change; my accent didn't disappear. I simply started to understand how I could communicate and influence others using the best of two different cultures. As a result, I became uniquely valuable in corporate America and, hopefully, a trailblazer for the next generation of Hispanics in STEM.

BIOGRAPHY

From a Catalan family, born in Puerto Rico, and living in Ohio, Miguel Alemany earned his engineering degree from the University of Puerto Rico. A forty-year R&D veteran of Procter & Gamble, he worked in every business unit before retiring as VP of R&D. Miguel is currently the Chair of the Board and interim CEO for SHPE. He is a tireless advocate for Hispanic issues, an in-demand public speaker, and a trainer on differences in work environment between Anglos and Hispanics. Fluent in three languages and able to function in seven, Miguel has a passion for travel and culture. An avid car enthusiast and race car driver, he believes stress disappears once you pass 180 mph.

KARA ALFONSO

"The more you share, the more you get back."

I was born and raised in the Bronx—and yes, it is everything you think it is. It was a tough place that in turn taught me to be tough. It made me strong and stubborn. I won't say that I flourished in that environment, but it formed me.

My parents both poured all that they had into me and my sisters. My mother established a strong desire to do what was right and a real love of reading and learning in us, while my father taught us to crave a sense of adventure and curiosity about the world. Those gifts formed me as well.

As I grew up, I used that stubbornness and I pushed myself to achieve. I went to private school, got into a private college, and got a good job. But working in a highly corporate environment was very intimidating. I felt like a misanthrope; I didn't belong. I was surrounded by doctors and scientists and statisticians. I was none of those things, but I was a good listener.

In my twenties, I was working in a very technical job when I was assigned to train a group of system users at a workshop. The workshop was in Kuala Lumpur. I had to check a map to see where that even was! At that point, the furthest east I had been from the Bronx was London.

I was very excited for this new experience, but also pretty scared. I did all the necessary research on customs in Malaysia— women should keep their shoulders covered, pointing was very rude, never show the soles of your feet, and so much more. I tried to remember it all. The workshop had attendees from twenty countries throughout Asia.

On the first day of the workshop, my co-facilitator stood at the front. She recognized a bit of tension in the room and started with an icebreaker, asking all in attendance to share a cultural tradition that is important to each of us.

As we went around the room and each attendee shared a bit about themselves and their culture, you could feel the tension leaving the room. "Ahh, I can be myself, my whole self," I thought to myself. The cultural nuances weren't being ignored but were being celebrated—and these differences were our starting point.

As everyone shared, we found commonalities that served for a lively dinner conversation after the work was done. This moment was so formative for me in my career. I came in feeling like an outsider and realized that so many others felt the same way. I learned that the more you share, the more you get back. Now it is so critical to my leadership style, and I lead with people in mind first.

BIOGRAPHY

Kara Alfonso was born in the Bronx to an artist/scientist and crafter/secretary. She was raised with various academic and cultural influences. In 1985, she was accepted into the Prep for Prep program, where she transitioned from public school in the Bronx to a private school in Manhattan. This jumpstart helped provide her with the foundation to eventually go to Wesleyan University where she earned a BA in Art History.

Armed with an art history degree, she worked her way into Pfizer Inc. as a systems analyst, arguing that the analytical nature of art history—which explores visual, historical, economic, and social aspects of art—would translate into system development.

She worked for several pharmaceutical companies over her twenty-five-year tenure and currently heads the regulatory solutions department at Pfizer, focused on bringing information-driven solutions to the regulatory department. She has continued to keep people at the heart of her work, driving efficiency, value, and improving overall user experience.

WHY YOUTHS MATTER

MIGUEL ANGULO

"God always paves the road for you and equips you with skills you will use in the future."

It wasn't the American Dream that brought me here to America, but the desire to help my family through their grief. My sister and her two kids tragically lost their husband and father in the American Airlines crash that took place in Colombia on December 20,1995. They were visiting us for Christmas.

My sister needed help and asked me to live with her to help her with her little ones. I never imagined how my life would change and, more importantly, how this situation helped me to build the skills I now use as a youth leader.

I have been youth leader for the past eighteen years. Oftentimes I asked myself, "Why does doing this matter so much to you?" Children are our present and the future of our nation.

But unfortunately, children are not able to develop their full potential on their own. Their dreams are truncated because they do not feel safe at home, at school, or the city where they live. They face many challenges. They feel lost, rejected, hated, fearful, and hopeless. They come to youth groups because they need to feel loved. They love when we attend their extracurricular activities. They feel secure knowing we pray for them. They lose their fears by engaging in activities like singing or playing instruments. They feel valued because everything they do matters to others. They feel empowered because they transform the lives of others.

I feel blessed because I am part of the transformations they experience every week. Working with them made me realize that God always paves the road for me and equips me with skills I will use in the future.

In 2019, I had the opportunity to travel on a ten-day mission trip to Guadalajara, Mexico, to work with youth groups. I visited an orphanage and engaged with the kids. I visited a rehab place for young men and women recovering from drug and alcohol addictions. While I was there, I stepped outside of my comfort zone.

I performed a play my team prepared for them, and later we sang and danced the songs we prepared for the younger kids. I still remember the expressions on their faces—they loved it. They got up from their chairs and started dancing and singing with us. We were able to bring them hope and joy.

For ten days, I dedicated my time to others, and I understood how rewarding it is to genuinely serve others. I am a cybersecurity engineer for Check Point Software Technologies, and I help clients build solutions to protect their companies from cyberattacks.

Likewise, I see the importance of working with these young people and helping them build foundational blocks that will make them feel safe. Regardless of what we do for a living, it is important to serve others. I invite you to be an advocate for people that do not have a voice, that are weak and tired and in slavery. Are you ready to influence others and transform their lives so future generations will have a better place to live?

BIOGRAPHY

Miguel Angulo is an engineer of cybersecurity at Check Point Software Technologies and focuses on datacenter and cloud security. As trusted advisor, Miguel works with clients, resellers, and distributors on solutions to protect companies from cyberattacks.

Miguel volunteers as a youth leader at Evangel Church in New Jersey and has gone on mission trips to work with youth. Miguel is also co-founder of MAS Connection and leads the Hispanic Star NJ Hub with his wife Adriana.

Miguel loves cooking, especially asados, even in the winter; Miguel has a passion for soccer, and he cheers for Barcelona FC.

ANNIE ANLAS

*"I had seen how much of a fighter my daughter had been, and
that motivated me to work even harder."*

I was getting my twenty-week sonogram—that's when the doctor tells you the sex of the baby. As the nurse was moving the machine around my belly, she told me I was going to have a girl. At that moment tears ran down my cheeks. I was ecstatic. Then she continued, saying, "Wait right here; I'm going to get the doctor." My heart sank.

The doctor came back, and he told me that one of my daughter's kidneys had too much fluid and that I would have to be monitored closely.

When my daughter was born, the excess liquid turned out to be a medical issue that needed multiple surgeries. I knew my daughter needed me, and I decided to dedicate my time to her. I quit my job as an art director and took care of her full-time. I still had the monetary responsibilities of splitting all costs, plus the medical bills.

As the months went by, I had to be resourceful and find a way to make ends meet. I used up all my savings, cashed out my 401K, and looked for extra ways to make money. I opened a design studio and designed for clients, sold clothes on eBay, signed up to be a mock juror, was a mystery shopper, and attended multiple focus groups. While my daughter was having surgeries, I managed to continue to support my family and keep us afloat.

Two years passed. My daughter had the surgeries she needed and she was finally healthy. I was able to go back into the workforce full-time. I started freelancing for only two weeks at Grubhub. As I got my foot in the door, I took on as many projects as I could.

My manager called me back again and again, each time with larger projects. I told myself that if I was going to be away from my daughter for even a second, it better be for a good reason—it better be for me to grow in my career, for her to have me as a role model, and for me to accomplish everything that we want.

As I continued working, I saw how the traits that I learned during those difficult years translated into my work. By being resourceful, determined, juggling multiple tasks, being a problem solver, and being optimistic, I was elevated in the company. I had seen how much of a fighter my daughter had been, and that motivated me to work even harder.

What started out as two weeks of helping out a team turned into co-managing a creative team in New York and Chicago for a global tech company. In a time of struggle, I achieved a sense of strength and confidence of knowing that I was able to accomplish what I wanted and overcome what was in my way. I acquired tools not just personally, but professionally as well. After everything that happened, I realized that it was in my darkest moments that I grew into the person I am today.

BIOGRAPHY

Annie Anlas is an associate creative director at Seamless/ Grubhub. Growing up in Peru, she was always captivated by her father's work as a creative director, and always knew it was what she wanted to do.

Annie earned her BBA in Strategic and Design Management at the prestigious Parsons School of Design. With over fifteen years of experience at leading New York agencies and companies, her expertise ranges across a wide range of disciplines, including branding, digital, print, advertising, and creative direction. Meanwhile, her experience spans the consumer-facing, publishing, technology, entertainment, pharmaceutical, and beauty industries, where she has received multiple awards.

PALENQUE

DR. MAYDA ANTUN

"Embracing opportunities and having success often lie in your ability to adapt."

I was born and raised in Tampa, Florida by Cuban immigrant parents. Growing up, I had never traveled outside the United States except for a family trip to Cuba before Communism scourged the island. Then in the late 1970s, my brothers and I moved to the Dominican Republic to attend medical school. My parents sold their treasured home to pay for our tuition.

The medical school I attended was part of a new university, founded not only to prepare professionals technically, but to educate them to fulfill the social needs of the communities they served. After the second year of medical school, the curriculum included working in a rural clinic for six months, residing in that community and facing some of the same challenges and experiences the community experienced.

My brothers and I were assigned to live in Palenque, where we rented a home which was excellent by local standards because it had an indoor shower; however, there was no toilet, just an outhouse.

Using his Marine Corps skills, my brother Marcial "renovated" the outhouse; and my brother Mario, having learned from my father—a carpenter and Renaissance man—brought running water into the kitchen.

We worked in the clinic in the mornings supervised by a physician. We had obtained sample medications from pharmaceutical companies and infant milk formula, and I had organized these in the clinic. We were so pleased to supply these to the community. In the afternoons, we treated emergencies, administered immunizations, and visited homes for a survey and census.

The living and sanitation conditions in many of the patient homes we visited caused concern and trepidation. Because of this, we devoted time to educating the patients and residents in the area. The patients were so grateful, inviting us to wonderful meals in their humble homes and bringing us delicious gifts, such as cherries, papayas, and chickens.

Nighttime and sleep were always an adventure. Slathered in insect repellant, laying in a cot under a mosquito net, I could hear the neighbor's donkey braying and the croaking of the frogs in the nearby pond. I would pass the time thinking about the patients I had treated, the ones who would get better, and the few who would not.

When the six-month rural rotation came to an end, we were humbled as the village came out to the streets to bid us farewell.

I will always remember sitting in the back of our jeep, leaving Palenque for the last time, looking at the street full of patients and friends waving goodbye. There was sadness, but I also felt fulfilled, not only for the care we had brought to this community, but for the lessons I had learned.

I saw firsthand how adaptability, openness, and being malleable were keys to our success in Palenque. I firmly believe that success often lies with a person's ability to adapt to new work environments and situations. The opportunities are truly endless when you take on this mindset.

BIOGRAPHY

Dr. Mayda Antun is a physician executive and a leader in clinical operations in managed care and provider organizations, with expertise in chronic care programs, performance management, service improvement, and strategic planning. She is the Chief Clinical Officer of CareMax, Inc.

Dr. Antun has worked for national organizations, such as United Healthcare and Humana, as a plan medical director and also leading physician group practices. She was one of Humana's top 100 leaders.

She holds an MBA degree from the University of Miami. In 2010, Dr. Antun was honored by her medical school as a Distinguished Alumnus.

DIANA ANZALDUA

"What an honor it is to have the opportunity to help others heal and access their full potential."

My name is Diana Anzaldua, and I was born and raised in Texas by two Latinx, first-generation teenage parents. Because being a teenage parent in my culture is cyclical, I was raised in an abusive, alcoholic, poor, and dysfunctional environment.

This would eventually lead me on a path of continuing the cycle by becoming a teen parent when I got pregnant at the age of thirteen and again at fifteen years old. I ultimately abandoned my childhood to be a mother, which I do not regret. I sacrificed my education as a new mom and stopped going to school after the eighth grade. I eventually began living on my own at age sixteen.

Somewhere through those first few years of being a teen mom and not fully realizing what it meant to be a responsible mother, I started to have anxiety and depression. This was when I finally began to realize those physical reactions I was experiencing were from the childhood trauma I endured, as well as the new expectations of being a teen mom and working adult while caring for two small children. I had to keep going—all while avoiding and ignoring the cues and signals from my body—for my children. No one told me that this is what it was like to live in survival mode.

Before I started seeing a therapist, I didn't even know what mental health was. I just knew that we didn't talk about it in my family because "*no estás loca.*" The stigma around mental illness was embarrassing. Could I trust someone—would they even be able to help me?

Therapy became an on-again and off-again process for an entire decade, with each time ending in internalized shame and judgement. Eventually, I found a therapist who looked like me. Finally, I found someone who I could feel safe with; someone who saw me and understood what it was like to be in a brown body. During my therapy process, I learned to embrace my struggles and culture and use it as my resilience.

Growing up in an abusive, low-income household exposed me to barriers I've learned to conquer. I've been on both sides. I've been a therapy client, as well as a therapist. Being a trauma therapist allows me the humbling honor of being on the front lines, making a difference in the lives of those suffering through similar inequities. "What an honor it is to have the opportunity to help others heal and access their full potential," I would constantly think to myself.

This eventually led me to create a trauma center in hopes of healing the wounds of generational trauma. My experience helped me realize that culturally relevant mental healthcare is needed in communities where there is so much historical and generational trauma. My healing would not have been possible had it not been for therapy.

Now, as a licensed psychotherapist, I believe that we are all deserving of healing. This can be a powerful transformational healing experience and a journey to healthy brain and body functioning and overall wellness.

BIOGRAPHY

Diana Anzaldua, the founder of Austin Trauma Therapy Center and Contigo Wellness, is a social change activist and trauma survivor. She knows the path to healing can be complex and challenging.

Her vision and leadership create a safe space for other survivors to grow, embrace their resilience, and heal—all in community with others. Diana's mission is to bring healing, financially accessible mental health care, and individual restoration, so communities everywhere can become the healthy, thriving, and inspiring individuals they were each created to be. Her belief is that if individuals thrive, this can also transform and uplift communities to thrive as a whole.

DON'T RELAX YOUR HAIR—IT WILL WALK YOU TOWARDS YOUR DESTINY

SULMA ARZU-BROWN

"My destiny is to finally bring together the Afro-Latino diaspora as we embrace our history and celebrate our authentic selves."

My name is Sulma. I am a proud Garifuna from Honduras. We are the Black Caribs forcibly deported from the islands of St. Vincent and the Grenadines in 1797 after the British assassinated our chief, Joseph Chatoyer. Their plans for genocide and slavery failed. The Garifuna people ended up in Honduras, eventually spreading to Guatemala, Belize, Nicaragua, and the United States. An estimated 250 thousand Garifuna live in New York.

Since I was born in Honduras, this also makes me an Afro-Latina. Although my history is impressive, what's even more dynamic is the spirt of resilience it left within our people. However, the challenges that plagued my ancestors would attempt its blows on my Mami.

Mami came to this country in the early 1980s because the financial institution she worked for refused to promote a Black,

Garifuna woman. The USA was her only hope at the success she dreamt of and the success she was qualified for. My father trusted her and followed her lead. They accomplished their goal of moving, and my brother joined them in the Bronx a few years later.

Despite the new challenges of growing up in the South Bronx, I graduated college, got a good job, married a man like my dad, and built a home for my family. My parents saw that their sacrifice was not in vain.

We went all out to assimilate, even straightening our hair—we were safe now! But the challenges that plagued my mom as an Afro-Latina would attempt to set its claws on me.

The summer of 2013 was hot and humid. I touched up my new hair growth with a relaxer every six weeks. But walking to the hair salon felt different that day. As I looked in the mirror, I was empowered to utter the words that would transform my life: "Cut my hair off!"

I was welcomed into my destiny with the most beautiful compliment I've ever heard, "I like your 'natural.'" I felt authentically respected. Most of those acknowledgements came from the Afro-Diaspora.

I did not realize how deeply rooted disdain for blackness was in the Latino community until the colloquial term *"pelo malo"* was used by my caregiver to describe my daughter's tight, curly afro. In a non-malicious tone, she advised I chemically straighten it.

My mommy defense mode went from zero to a hundred! As my daughter firmly set her eyes on me, I chose to respond with love. I promised to find a book that would elevate the self-esteem of all the children under her care. I didn't find one authentic to my experience. God gifted me with creating the children's book *Pelo Malo No Existe!/Bad Hair Does Not Exist!*

That hot summer day proved that my spirit was ready for another type of new growth. I am now a part of a beautiful revolution that brings honor to my ancestors and the sacrifice of parents. My destiny is to finally bring together the Afro-Latino diaspora as we embrace our history and celebrate our authentic selves.

BIOGRAPHY

For over fifteen years, Sulma Arzu-Brown has been working as a champion for diversity and inclusion, well before the term became a trending topic.

Sulma's work with The Garifuna Coalition USA and NYC Hispanic Chamber of Commerce has merited her many award recognitions.

She is the author of the award-winning book *Bad Hair Does Not Exist!/Pelo Malo No Existe!* and *My Hair Comes With Me: Shifting the Paradigm of What Success Looks Like!* She is the creator of the nation's first Afro-Latino sitcom TV series entitled D'QUE LATINO. She utilizes her platform to bring honor to the Afro-Latino Diaspora.

MADELINE BACHELIER

"The adversity I faced reveals how much I care about uplifting my community, because it is my faith and community that pulls me up to move forward."

My parents always say *"mija,* you're going to be somebody." I still wonder what "somebody" means. I could not help but think of these words while wrapping up my night shift at the local cupcake shop I worked at growing up. As I shifted my mop back and forth, my mind flopped with it, each movement a new, frustrating thought. I often wondered, "Why am I here? Is this what it meant to be somebody?"

Growing up, I was a three-sport athlete. After college I started my first position with a professional baseball team, ecstatic and energized. I struggled; oftentimes I was subject to Latina stereotypes but proved myself when I volunteered to be the only active Spanish speaker assisting Hispanic fans to buy tickets. Though my Spanish is average, I speak it to let people know without a doubt that I am proud of my Mexican heritage. To prove myself at this job, in this way, I really felt like I was finding my path to be the "somebody" my parents always talked about.

Eventually, I was ready to leave my job working in professional baseball. This transitional period was the most challenging time in my life, yet somehow, I still knew it was important. At that time, I was living with a childhood friend of mine, a fellow Latina in my community, who understood. I lived there rent-free and slept in her living room on an air mattress. In four months, I saved enough to finally put in my two weeks.

My mental health was weak, but I found strength through my faith, family, and friends. One day when I was folding laundry right before my afternoon shift, I was thinking about a fellowship position I had interviewed for in New York. By that point I told myself to move on; nevertheless, the thought still permeated in my mind, drawing me in like the smell of cupcakes often drew in customers. As I was folding my clothes, I looked up, tears already welling and said, "God, take me anywhere and I will follow you with full faith and confidence."

Suddenly, the phone rang.

"Ms. Bachelier?"

"Yes?"

"Hi, I'm calling to congratulate you and offer you the Partnerships Fellow position here in New York City!"

Living in this city has given me perspective to answer what it means to be "somebody," especially as a Mexican American woman. I had been seeking a sense of purpose and sometimes, belonging.

Coincidentally, I found out about *Hispanic Star* from another strong Latina in my circle. My lesson? There will be times where you want to give up on yourself, when you wonder if you are somebody. To be somebody, I have discovered, means to be proud of your roots. As Latinas, we have to lift each other up, remind each other that we move with grace, intention, and ambition. The adversity I faced reveals how much I care about uplifting my community, because it is my faith and community that pulls me up to move forward.

BIOGRAPHY

Madeline Bachelier grew up in Arizona by the US and Mexico border, where she embraced the value of two cultures with her family and friends. At an early age, she was taught the importance of community, empathy, and compassion, and holds these as her guiding values throughout her life.

In 2017, she graduated from the University of Arizona and majored in marketing. Madeline moved to New York City in 2019, where she learned to adapt to another lifestyle with perseverance and agility. She intends to have community and social impact as focal points throughout her career, especially in sports and entertainment.

HOW FINDING MY IDENTITY
HELPED ME ELEVATE MY VOICE

DR. HUMBERTO BAQUERIZO

"My voice and being present have allowed me to have a seat at the table."

My immigrant journey started off similar to many of those who seek new beginnings. I came to the United States from Ecuador, and grew up in Union City, NJ. I attended Memorial High School in West New York, NJ, and then NJIT in Newark, NJ, under the Educational Opportunity Fund.

Being raised by a divorced mother, I quickly learned the relevance social determinants of health had on my own life. At times, my family was dependent on public assistance. To help my mother, I worked at a local bodega in merchandising, as a clerk, and as a *carnicero* (butcher) during my high school years. These jobs allowed me to see firsthand the challenges faced by immigrants.

My time at Univision gave me a greater understanding of my cultural identity. Through work, I was able to participate in parades, sales/marketing presentations, and help develop the power of the Hispanic vote. But although I found my identity, I struggled to find my voice.

At this point in my life, I felt odd; I had a secure job, a successful career at NJIT, amazing family and friends. Yet, my doctoral degree at Caldwell University, where I studied resilience and grit among minority students in STEM shed light on a different story: many others like me were still left behind.

I recognized the lack of minority representation in STEM, and that degree completion is much lower for Latino males. I encountered similar stories while overseeing Rutgers New Jersey Medical School pipeline programs for underrepresented and/or socioeconomically disadvantaged college and high school students. Our students truly had shown the potential for excellence but may not have had the social capital or displayed the resilience needed to be competitive applicants. Participating in each student's journey helped me recognize that academic skills, coupled with motivation, resilience/grit, and mentorship, could be the winning formula for these students to succeed. While I have not found my voice, I have found my purpose.

I recall a particular story of a mentee, a Latino student whom I was able to relate to. He inspired me to create Mentor U Connect, an organization that helps youth learn the social-emotional skills necessary to succeed. I now know that my voice has an impact, my story can inspire others, and my mentorship can help change their narrative. My voice and being present has allowed me to have a seat at the table, break down barriers, close the educational gap, and improve health equity for underserved populations.

As leaders, we must find and use our voices for hardworking families, for small businesses—like the immigrant bodega employees who took care of me when my family struggled to make ends meet—and for all of those who feel invisible in society. Our diverse voices matter and are tired of being invisible in the community and the political process. Find your purpose and discover your unique voice, because it has a more prolonged impact in serving those who are invisible to our society.

BIOGRAPHY

Dr. Humberto Baquerizo is the CEO/President of Mentor U Connect and the Hispanic Affair Commissioner for the City of Newark. He co-founded and is a team member of the Cancer Health Justice Lab (CHJL) at Rutgers School of Public Health, a community ambassador for University Hospital, and a program/educational specialist at Rutgers New Jersey Medical School.

Dr. Baquerizo has a Doctoral Degree in Educational Leadership from Caldwell University, an MBA from the University of Phoenix, and a BS in Engineering Science from NJIT. His research interests include social determinants of health, student success, grit, resilience, and underrepresented minorities pipeline initiatives.

LANGUAGE IMMERSION MAKES A DIFFERENCE

STEPHANIE BAZAN

"Without an understanding of the Spanish language, I never would have discovered the beauty of a world and people I can proudly call my own."

I moved to Buenos Aires, Argentina in 1995 with an imperfect understanding of Spanish and a lack of international business experience—a recipe for many awkward and embarrassing moments. Mispronounced or misused words implied a different meaning than what I had intended, often resulting in feelings of inadequacy during casual conversations or business presentations.

But, as with any full immersion, my Spanish skills blossomed during my time in Latin America—and it became the skill that would most alter the course of my life.

Equipped with a way to communicate with those around me, I noticed myself becoming more and more like the locals. I dropped English entirely and picked up the local accent and colloquialisms. I adapted to local fashions. I let my hair grow. I listened to their music. I traveled to learn the culture and histories embedded in the Latin American people. I became one of them—and they became part of me. Because I could connect with its people through a common language, Latin America's cities, countries, and the continent itself took on a whole new beauty.

I returned to the United States four years later to find that, for as much as I had changed, a lot had changed here, too. Namely, Hispanic culture had finally infused itself into the American tapestry—socially, economically, and professionally. All of a sudden, Spanish-speaking cultural talent experts were high in demand to represent the voice of the Hispanic consumer. As someone who had worked hard to find her voice among Spanish speakers, I knew the importance of this kind of communication and decided to pursue it as a profession.

It was not an easy go at first. Most of the time it was a job performed in isolation, but I was committed to giving a voice to a demographic that was so important to me. My personal experience abroad taught me the fundamental understanding of how cultural cues, traditions, and heritage play such an important role in the lives of U.S Hispanics. That translates directly to how they interact with brands, consume media, and connect with one another.

In this way, the work I do positively impacts local Hispanic communities in the US by providing them with a sense of the familiar. On the other side of the coin are those in Latin American countries who work hard to sustain their families and community— especially those in Mexico who cultivate one of the world's most beloved fruits. The rich cultural experiences I was immersed in those years ago are being shared through my work in the Hispanic space. And without an understanding of the Spanish language, I never would have discovered the beauty of a world and people I can proudly call my own.

BIOGRAPHY

Stephanie Bazan leads the shopper and trade marketing areas for Avocados From Mexico (AFM). Under her leadership and strategic vision, AFM has driven Mexican avocado demand and accelerated the fruit's popularity to record levels.

As a bilingual professional with more than twenty years of marketing experience in domestic and international markets, she has extensive experience in many industries, including food and beverage, entertainment, and retail.

Stephanie has an MBA in International Marketing from the University of Dallas, a BA from NYU, and continuing education certificates from Yale University, the Kellogg School of Management at Northwestern University, and Stanford University.

JOE A. BERNARD

"Never be afraid to show your true self, as the many colors of your culture will shine through toward your eventual success."

When I was seven years old, I remember my mother in the kitchen washing the dishes after having cooked a full meal. At around 8 p.m., she stopped what she was doing and ran into the living room upon hearing an opening title sequence that introduced two motorcycled police officers riding on a California freeway. My mother would come over to me and whisper in my ear. *"Tú ves ese hombre,"* She would say while pointing to Erik Estrada. *"Él es como tú!"*

Ironically, when I entered the professional world of advertising in 1988, the meaning of those words my mom said began to have greater significance.

I was constantly rushing out of my house to ensure I got to the office early. The 125-year-old advertising agency had a commodore founder that resembled the *Titanic* captain.

I had a forty-five-minute subway commute. In the summer, it

was so hot that I often commuted dressed down but changed into business attire upon arriving. In those days, there were no electronic pass keypads, so I had a basic key—and I'd left mine in my top drawer that day. Unfortunately, I had to wait 25 minutes in the elevator bank until someone came along.

At 8:45 a.m., an older lady who sat half a hallway away from me got off the elevator and I immediately felt the tension. I tried to break the ice with a smile and a familiar, "Oh so glad you are here, as I forgot my key." Her response was earth shattering to me, as she said, "Well, you realize that you are on the fourth floor. The mailroom is on the second floor." Immediately, my heart sank to my feet. I was managing conflicting emotions of being completely offended and trying to stay professional. I said, "Lady, I work on this floor, in the media department. My office is around the corner from yours." The woman stopped and then I think she recognized me or was embarrassed for making a drastic assumption. She opened the door and we both went our separate ways.

As I think about that moment, I understand that she was only reacting to what she knew. The concept of *"Él es como tú"* didn't exist for her, as many Latinos were not in her line of work. It's a moment that I would never forget, and that would spur me on in my career to be included, visible, and effective.

But this isn't the only story like this. I have a million of 'em. These moments when my character was tested only brought to mind the genius of my mother's programming. Her early attempt to underscore my value and remind me that I had a place has fueled my career, no matter the odds.

Today we have a saying: "Why not us?" It similarly unpins my ambitions to succeed and show the world coming up behind that we all have place in the hierarchy of business and the world stage. As many have said, this Latino marketplace is the most engaging, vibrant, and colorful universe, with rhythms, arts, and smarts to match. We are all blessed to have this common connection with one another, and we should continue to support each other in all our endeavors. Someone out there might be looking at us and whispering to themselves, *"Son como yo!"*

BIOGRAPHY

Joe A. Bernard is a top media executive with marketing and sales experience in both mature and startup entertainment media companies. He is an owner, partner, and chief revenue officer at NGL Collective, a leading digital media and entertainment company serving the US Latinx marketplace. At NGL Collective, Joe leads revenue and partnership relationships for the company.

He was born in Harlem, NY, and lives in NJ with his wife and three sons. Joe's career milestones include leading revenue for Mun2 at NBCU, where he recreated Pepsi Música, the one-hour music show, and launched I Love Jenni with superstar Jenni Rivera.

CECILE BLANCARTE

"Is it just me, or do all Latina mothers shame their daughters into defiance?"

Escandalosa is how my mom describes me. I've also heard her call me *sinvergüenza* and *terca*. That last word made me leave her house fuming mad one day. I thought it meant stupid until I looked it up—hahaha! I guess it wasn't so bad. Ohh, us poor Latinas. Is it just me, or do all Latina mothers shame their daughters into defiance? Lucky for me, this shaming became my power shake. Thanks to my Latina mom, my life is defined by the sum of many defining moments and not just one power shake. It's the sum of being *escandalosa, sinvergüenza,* and *terca*.

Escandalosa—This is me at the age of nineteen, deciding to live in Puerto Vallarta and Cancun for almost two years and sell timeshares. *Escandalosa* is what my mom called me when I shipped out to Puerto Vallarta. I learned so much about sales while in Mexico! The one downside about this time in my life was the boyfriend. He did all he could to squash my independence and passion for success. I escaped by calling my Mom and asking her to get me a flight back to California.

Sinvergüenza—This is me at twenty-four, getting into one of the best engineering colleges, Cal Poly San Luis Obispo, through a back door! I was denied admission and then I decided to make a phone call to the College of Natural Resources Management. I told them about my electronic mapping experience, and they accepted me into their program. Six months later, I transferred into the College of Engineering. *"Ay, sinvergüenza"* my mom called me, once I told her how I made it into the environmental engineering program.

Terca—When I first started my business, my mom called me this. I initially misinterpreted it for meaning stupid. I get it now. I had a full-time job as an engineer and was suddenly furloughed during the 2007 Great Recession. So, what did I decide to do? I created a beach concierge business, Beach Butlerz, that eventually bloomed into a high-end experience event staging business and had a second offshoot called Butlerz Events. I kept my engineering job throughout the whole experience and sold Beach Butlerz eight years later at its peak revenue.

I'm excited about my next business venture. I look forward to all the defining moments along the way. It's about paving a road for all Latinx to follow. It's my turn to be the shoulders for them to stand on. How does my mom feel about this new venture? Well, her exact words were, *"Qué barbaridad!"* Her reason? She says most people at my age are planning their retirement and not starting a new business. All I can say is: *"Gracias,* mom for giving me reasons to prove otherwise."

I wish all my Latinx community to live a life full of defining moments, or as my mom would put it, as *barbaridades, escandalosos, sinvergüenzas,* and *tercas. Estoy a sus órdenes.*

BIOGRAPHY

Cecile Blancarte is the founder and the creative mind behind the Latinx-inspired luxury brand, Blancarte. She provides high-end, technology-enabled fashion, accessories, and home interiors. Cecile has led the prosperous launch of Blancarte through her belief in servant leadership, her passion for people, and her work to ensure her business and our planet thrive.

CANCIONES DE LA TIERRA

SOFIA BORK

"These plants represent knowledge passed down through generations, a song of the earth that is reclaimed and honors a people who themselves have journeyed far, a story echoed in my family heritage."

"Tomate, pimento verde," my grandmother known as "Mimi" to her fourteen grandchildren softly murmurs, as she points to the delicate plants, steadily growing in defiance of the muggy Georgia heat. Nestled in the foothills of the North Georgia mountains, my hometown of Dahlonega was full of happy memories spent wandering the forest and growing in tandem with nature.

The soft lilt of my mother and Mimi's voices in Spanish carried with the mountain breeze instilled a feeling of happiness as my sister and I played by the garden. Years later, when I first visited my mother's hometown of Bogotá, Colombia, I remember the vibrancy of the flowers and understood my Mimi's passion for gardening, a gentle melody always present in my heart.

The move from the mountains to the city of Atlanta, Georgia was jarring for me. Atlanta's roads were narrow; I missed home and the starry, still nights—nature's symphony. However, I acclimated quickly and became involved with a variety of community organizations.

In 2018, the opportunity to meld my love of gardening and my Latin heritage sprouted when Isabel Gonzalez Whitaker asked if I would help create a community garden in a local Atlanta park called the Sara J. Gonzalez Memorial Park. The park was named after Isabel's mother, who was an Atlanta civic and community leader, and it is the only park in Georgia named after a Latinx person. Though I had no prior experience working with city planning or permitting, the ability to create a garden in a park that authentically reflected the surrounding community was inspiring.

This community garden is ethnobotanical, meaning all the plants are indigenous to Central and South America, and were sourced from the University of Georgia's Latin American Ethnobotanical Garden. The park is named after Officer Edgar I. Flores, who was the first Latinx police officer to be shot in line of duty in the city of Atlanta. The Officer Edgar I. Flores Memorial Latinx Ethnobotanical Garden was officially unveiled in October of 2019, in a ceremony attended by Edgar's family as well as city and community leaders.

The garden is tended by local community volunteers, many of whom are immigrants themselves. Edgar's family are regular attendees, and each year, they are gifted a plant from the garden to take home and plant in their garden. This year, the Agave sprouted two "pups," which are offshoots, and were presented to Edgar's family. Agave plants are frequently used in horticultural therapy to help people process the loss of a loved one, since the "pups" grow far from the "mother" plant, yet the root systems remain interconnected. Not only does the garden memorialize the sacrifice of Officer Flores, but it directly preserves Latinx cultural knowledge. Community volunteers enthusiastically recount stories of yerba mate, tomatillos, and other plants. These plants represent knowledge passed down through generations, a song of the earth that is reclaimed and honors a people who themselves have journeyed far, a story echoed in my family heritage.

BIOGRAPHY

Sofia Bork is Latina and employed as a Readiness Specialist with Truist. She is the founder of the Officer Edgar I. Flores Memorial Latinx Ethnobotanical Garden in the Sara J. Gonzalez Park, the first park in Georgia named after a person of Latinx descent.

She is a recipient of the "50 Most Influential Latinos in Georgia" award for both 2019 and 2020, presented by the Georgia Hispanic Chamber of Commerce. In her advocacy of equitable and accessible greenspaces, she received the Park Pride 2020 Inspiration Award. Sofia earned a Bachelors in English Writing and Publication from the University of North Georgia.

DAVID BREZLER

"Maintain an open mind and an entrepreneurial spirit."

In 2012, a week before election day, on Halloween weekend, something that had only happened once before in the recorded history of the city of New York happened: Hurricane Sandy slammed into the five boroughs with astounding force and created a nightmare situation for everyone.

I was living in Westchester then, working on a local election campaign to survive the recession. We hunkered down, making sure we had plenty of water and nonperishable food until the power could be restored, and finally all made it back to the normalcy of personal interactions and mobilizing around the community after the weekend. I still have pictures of miles-long lines of cars waiting to enter gas stations to fill up because several ran out of reserves. Fuel supply barges had ridden out the storm at sea and couldn't dock for three days.

In the storm's aftermath, FEMA deployed resources to New

York, but not before I had the opportunity to join a volunteer collective from a number of local unions who chartered a bus out to the Rockaways to do emergency support. I remember crossing the bridge and seeing blocks-long, two-stories-high piles of debris. Demolition machines bit off giant, yawning metal jaws full of material, depositing them onto trash barges to be floated away. The air was sour with smells of mold, soaked wood, and sea water. I had to stay in the warehouse and keep supplies organized, providing needs to everyone else while wearing a HEPA-filter mask the entire day—and even with respiratory protective equipment, breathing was difficult. I wasn't capable of diving into the houses and mucking out basements that had been flooded by the waves.

Shortly after that experience, I joined FEMA community outreach efforts into storm affected areas of Westchester County. (We learned there were many.)

A year later, another opportunity arose to leverage my Master of Public Administration Degree and National Urban Fellows training by joining a construction program management team rebuilding storm-affected public housing in New York City. During nearly seven years on the project, a lot happened for me both personally and professionally. I earned a Project Management Professional (PMP) certification, became a New York State Civil Service Project Manager II, completed Desktop Level III Tableau training, bought a co-op near my family, and supported my parents' COVID-19 survival. After both vaccines, I now proudly own my own business focusing on data analytics and project management.

To quote my father: "What is the teaching point?" *No hay*

bien que por mal no venga. Roughly translated: "No good deed goes unpunished." But, as sages often say, there are other interpretations: "Never miss an opportunity to capitalize on a good disaster" or, "Innovation happens when opportunity meets preparation." Another lesson: "Maintain an open mind, and an entrepreneurial spirit."

It doesn't mean purposefully cause yourself suffering. However, training—especially training that is strategic, timely, and leads to perennially utilizable skills—that is always worth the effort. Lastly, the mantra of a fitness supplier I use: "Don't quit. Ever."

BIOGRAPHY

David Brezler was born in the Bronx, NY. Prior to project management, he was a NYC Public School teacher, and translator/interpreter in medical and legal settings. He earned his Master of Public Administration from Baruch College and is also a National Urban Fellow. He was previously the executive vice president of the ALPFA New Jersey Chapter and still engages in leadership activities through his local Project Management Institute chapter, maintains an active fitness routine, and is a business owner.

CHALLENGES (AND HOW WE HANDLE
THEM) DEFINE US

ILSE CALDERON

*"Growing up, my parents instilled in me a strong desire to study
and never stop learning."*

I remember waking up at what must have been 3 a.m. After an eight-plus hour car ride from Mexico, we had just arrived in Houston, Texas: our new home. As my sisters and I began to settle into our new reality, we were wide-eyed at every corner we turned. We didn't know it then, but my parents had just sacrificed their life in Mexico to be able to give us the best gift they ever could have: an opportunity to begin school (and hopefully university) in the US.

At the time, I didn't understand what a big deal that had been. They didn't have a secure livelihood in Texas; and yet, they wholeheartedly believed the United States was the answer to a better future.

Growing up, my parents instilled a strong desire to study and never stop learning in me.

A common phrase in our household was "your schoolwork is

your job." However, that didn't

mean we weren't expected to also excel outside of school. During elementary school summers, we had daily four-hour readings my dad required. Back then, I despised this requirement; yet, I now credit it for having taught me the value of time. I would wake up early to make sure my readings didn't sit undone.

Even if my parents had to work multiple jobs, they always found a way to afford us

experiences that would help expand our minds. We did gymnastics, swimming club, and even acting classes. Years later, when it was time to apply for colleges, I was lost. I had always been a good student, but I knew it took more than that to get into a top-tier school. To this day, I am indebted to my parents, but especially my dad, for his endless research and advising my sisters and me on the best way to showcase ourselves. It was his idea that we do summer programs, become Rotary Youth exchange ambassadors, and start a volunteering club. It was my dad that encouraged us to apply (and ultimately enroll) at Stanford. I continue to be in awe of everything that he has done for us.

I could tell a hundred more stories about how my parents are amazing. No challenge left

them debilitated, whether it was losing a job, raising children without a community, or even losing my little brother (the light of all our lives) a year ago. The lesson here is about using your challenges as vehicles for growth. While it sounds cheesy, it is a lesson we should all strive to learn and live by.

I wish I had appreciated my parents' challenges and sacrifices earlier in life, because it completely changed the outcome of my life. I look back at my extended family in Mexico and realize the only difference between them and me is that I was lucky enough to have parents who took on so much more than was required of them to make sure I had more opportunities and for a better life.

BIOGRAPHY

Ilse Calderon is a principal at an early-stage venture capital firm, OVO Fund. She first joined OVO as an associate three years ago and has quickly moved up to principal. At OVO Ilse is part of a two-person team that sources and invests in ten to twelve start-ups per year that are raising their first round of capital.

Ilse spends a lot of time advocating her thesis, *The Rise of the Hypercultural Latinx*, that focuses on finding companies and founders that sell products, platforms, or services to the 20% of the US population who are Latinx.

ENDING THE LONG SEARCH FOR STABILITY

MARISA CALDERON

"I want to give these communities the opportunity to invest in their futures by feeling the stability and security of owning a home and enjoying the simple pleasures of hanging a painting on the wall without asking for permission."

Though I do not often talk about myself, I have come to realize that my upbringing has played a major role in the person I am today, both personally and professionally.

Both my grandfathers were part of the Bracero Program, which consisted of an agreement that allowed millions of Mexican men to come to the US seasonally to work on agricultural lands. My family was given the opportunity to come to this country, where we took full advantage of all there is to offer—including living in an owned home.

Although I was born in the US, my family's immigrant experience shaped my upbringing and directly impacted my perspective on building a stable future. I still consistently hear my mother's words each and every day: "This is how you are going to make your way, so you don't struggle like I do."

Growing up in Compton, known for its violent history with local gang activity in the late 1980s, my mother was always on the lookout for an opportunity to escape, aspiring to bigger opportunities. She eventually did escape and joined the military, where she would later meet her husband while they both served their country.

It was a thrill and an accomplishment when they returned to California and purchased a family home of their own, taking that all-important leap toward the financial and economic stability so many growing families strive for.

Not unlike many first- and second-generation Latino families, I was raised largely by my strong mother who demanded excellence and aspired to provide opportunities for her children that she herself was not afforded. Her good graces, coupled with my own success and hard work, allowed me to attend the University of California, Berkeley, where I had to take up a full-time job and a three-year academic leave to be able to pay for my studies. During this pause, I accidently stumbled upon the financial services sector, which, being an uncommon career choice among Latinos, presented its own opportunities and challenges.

After some time working in financial services, I transitioned into the real estate space, which is where I experienced most of my growth. This milestone allowed me to be more liberated toward who I was and who I was trying to create change for. I was passionate about my work without having to be an apologist about parts of myself that others did not come to understand.

In my new role as executive director of NCRC CDF, my aim is to pay it forward to other families and community members the same way my mom did for me. Through this fund, I work to build wealth and reduce poverty and unemployment in low- and moderate-income neighborhoods. I want to give these communities the opportunity to invest in their futures by feeling the stability and security of owning a home and enjoying the simple pleasures of hanging a painting on the wall without asking for permission. These communities need the same opportunities for homeownership to help stabilize their families for generations.

BIOGRAPHY

Marisa Calderon is the executive director of NCRC's Community Development Fund and a housing and financial services industry veteran. She has previously served on the advisory board for the Bank of California and the Fannie Mae Affordable Housing Advisory Council and authored the annual State of Hispanic Homeownership Report.

Marisa currently serves on the advisory board of Latinas Lead California and Hispanic Wealth Project, which has a stated goal of tripling the median household wealth of Hispanics by 2024. She earned her bachelor's degree from the University of California at Berkeley and is in the process of completing her MBA.

EDUCATION TRANSFORMED MY LIFE'S TRAJECTORY. NOW I'M GIVING BACK

ENEDINA CÁRDENAS

"Life's difficulties motivated me to find opportunities to grow and learn."

My story, like many others, reflects a combination of hard work and luck. My father was sent to the United States as a teenager to work in the fields and send money back to his family in Mexico, where my grandmother was raising the rest of her children. He didn't let his limited English ability and lack of higher education stop him.

My parents certainly instilled the importance of education in my brother and me. Growing up, I recall my parents placing a great weight on education. My dad always longed to complete college. I think my father's regret of not finishing college kept me focused to attend my dream school, UC Berkeley, after graduating high school. My brother and I represent a small minority of our extended family who pursued a graduate degree. It certainly changed our career trajectory.

I feel very fortunate for the opportunities I've been granted. I believe that it is my duty to not only excel in my profession, but to also use my platform as an attorney to fight for my community.

Mural de la Raza

Mural de la Raza was a mural painted in the late 1980's by muralist Jose Meza Velasquez. It depicted rich Hispanic culture and included depictions of the Mayans and Aztecs as well as prominent public figures like César Chávez. In August 2018, *Mural de La Raza* was painted over.

Mr. Velasquez's piece validated my community. Growing up, I didn't have access to books to learn about Mexican American culture in elementary school. I do remember seeing this mural every Sunday when we drove past it on the way to my uncle's house for family dinner. It was important to see reminders of my culture and heritage outside of my family circle, like that mural. I didn't realize what an impact it had on me until I learned that it had been painted over.

For me, the mural's erasure signaled more than just a loss of piece of artwork. It signaled the start of displacement of a culture, an inevitable byproduct of gentrification and redevelopment. I needed to do something to fight to save *La Raza*. I represented Mr. Velasquez in a civil suit to try to save *El Mural de la Raza*.

Fight for La Raza's Employment Rights

I am committed to continuing to fight for La Raza in my legal career. I am dedicated to representing Spanish-speaking clients who are taken advantage of at the workplace. I enjoy empowering Spanish-speaking workers on their labor rights and will continue to do so through the support of local community-based organizations. My dedication to my studies and pursuing higher education enriched my life. It is a joy to help my community through my profession.

BIOGRAPHY

Enedina Cárdenas is a civil litigator with a focus on business and employment matters. She co-founded Hansra Cardenas LLP to empower her clients by ensuring they understand their rights.

In 2016, Enedina was recognized in *Sacramento Magazine's* Top Lawyers List for Labor & Employment. She was recognized as a Northern California Super Lawyers Rising Stars in 2021 for the second consecutive year.

Enedina received her Bachelor of Arts degree from the University of California at Berkeley in Political Science. She received her law degree from Santa Clara University School of Law.

MY FAMILIA AS MY DAILY MOTIVATION IN LIFE

ENRIQUE CASTRO

"Being a Hispanic with a legal status and college education is a privilege, and it should grow in each one of us a sense of responsibility to care for our paisanos who did not have the fortune but are here anyway."

My *familia* has always been my biggest motivation. My fuel to keep going through the hard days and nights that life unexpectedly brings. I knew it but may have never realized it until 2016, when my younger brother was diagnosed with a brain tumor. I do not talk much about it, but I believe it was the trigger that led me to the United States, and it is what pushes me every day to work hard and be an advocate for my Hispanic community.

Before, I thought I had everything planned back home. As a numbers enthusiast with intellectual curiosity, I loved working as a public servant for the Mexican Government. I spent sixty hours a week designing public policy to reduce multidimensional poverty, increased the quality of education, upgraded the skills of our *paisanos* in the Mexican labor force, and promoted the creation of good-paying jobs in the poorest regions of the country.

But in light of my brother's medical condition, I did not think twice before changing my path to find better ways to support my *familia*, which ultimately brought me to Houston to pursue growth opportunities and entrepreneurship.

It was hard seeing my little brother go through a four-year period of hours-long surgeries, months at the hospital recovering, and a long journey of love, patience, and self-discovery. But his determination has taken him from signing together "Up&Up" on room 115 at the hospital, to being top of his class at marketing school—and he is a daily example that we can achieve whatever goal we set our minds to.

As an immigrant from Chiapas, the poorest state in Mexico, I often miss my *familia*. But every time I feel this way, I remember the mission that brought me here: to level the playing field for the Hispanic community through education. Education through my work, my voice, and my podcast in Spanish give back from the place of privilege where I am standing. Because being a Hispanic with a legal status and college education is a privilege.

And this privilege should grow a sense of responsibility in each one of us, to care for our paisanos who did not have the fortune but are here anyway. We should support all of those who came hoping for a better future for their families, even if they are exploited as day laborers, risk deportation every single day, and still work from sunrise to sunset to sunrise hoping to provide their families a better future.

As my story shows, our paths are rarely straight lines, and every decision we take in our lives defines who we are today. But I am not alone, and whatever our path is, our Hispanic community is one big *familia*—and our *familia* is counting on us to do our part. I encourage everyone to support our Hispanic community, no matter the age, gender, level of education, or stage in our lives; there is always something we can do for them. For us.

BIOGRAPHY

Enrique Castro is an economist that works to empower the Hispanic community through education. Based in Houston, TX, he has helped Hispanic businesses raise capital funding and adopt new technologies to scale their businesses.

Through his first company, BH Ventures, Enrique hosts a yearly accelerator program for Black and Hispanic founders. He is creator and host of the El Taco Financiero podcast, a weekly podcast in Spanish that promotes financial and business education, and together with his partner Zaira, created LatinXCoders to close the gap in STEM for Hispanic children. He has a beautiful husky named Margo and likes to play videogames.

THE IMPACT OF AN INFORMATIONAL INTERVIEW

EMMANUEL CAUDILLO

"Career plans can change, especially if unexpected events happen. Don't underestimate the importance of making a good first impression on an informational interview."

Serving in a position to help Hispanic students and families is a tremendous honor. I enjoy listening to stories, connecting people, and seeing Hispanic bright spots in action. Looking back, it was an informational interview that led me to this position.

My first full-time position was with the US Department of Education (DOE), where I worked as a budget analyst. It was a great position with fulfilling work, but my passion was working on Hispanic education policy. As a young professional, I was trying to navigate my career. I had begun creating a career plan, but I kept getting stuck on the next steps. To get unstuck, I joined a mentoring program at the DOE, where I was matched with an incredible mentor. She guided me in developing that plan and how I can work on Hispanic education policy.

During the mentoring season, she had presented to the White House Initiative. Thinking of me, she helped me get connected with the Initiative's leadership. After connecting with their deputy director, we arranged an informational interview.

I came into this informational interview not seeking a job, but to learn more about the Initiative. Knowing this opportunity was rare, I prepared myself for it by researching the latest Hispanic education statistics and developed questions I would ask the Initiative's deputy director.

During the informational interview, I learned what they did, how they accomplished their goals, and how they wanted to improve the educational outcomes of Hispanics. He also asked me questions about my thoughts on Hispanic education policy and my career goals. Afterwards, they connected me to their listserv and invited me to their upcoming events.

I felt accomplished after the interview and more importantly, I was surprised how much it connected to my own career goals. Now, I had a new goal, and that was to work with the Initiative. I thought that it would probably take a few years to reach that goal. But I was determined to align my progress in my career towards the Initiative while maintaining contact with them.

But life takes a twist. Unbeknownst to me, I had made an impression on him. Six months later, there was an opening with the Initiative and the former deputy director, now director, approached me and asked if I wanted to work with them. I was caught off guard with the offer.

And thus began my journey in working with the Initiative,

first as a detailee, later as a full-time staffer. It has been an incredible journey since then, and I have been able to live my passion by working on Hispanic education policy. This event in my life showed me two things: Career plans can change, especially if unexpected events happen, and the importance of making a good first impression on an informational interview. While an informational interview is information gathering, putting the work in the preparation and taking it seriously could lead to further opportunities down the road, some coming sooner than later.

BIOGRAPHY

Emmanuel Caudillo is the senior advisor to the White House Hispanic Prosperity Initiative. Prior to his current position, he was a budget analyst at the US Department of Education. He has also held research positions in various organizations, including Abt Associates and the National Council on Teacher Quality.

Emmanuel was named on the 40 Under 40 from the Leadership Center for Excellence in 2015 and 2019–2020 Excellence in Government Fellow at the Partnership for Public Service. Originally from Los Angeles, he holds a bachelor's degree from the University of Southern California and a Master of Public Policy from The George Washington University.

LISBETH CEBALLOS

"Once you learn that those are just lessons and you are enough, there is no stopping you!"

I am Lisbeth Ceballos; I was born in Venezuela and raised with lots of love. My father was raised as an orphan and valued family. He was married for sixty-two years and helped my mom raise five kids, became an engineer, and drilled the importance of education in all of us.

After graduating from high school, I came to the United States, alone, to study English and Hospitality Management. It was my dream. Being here was scary, especially not knowing anyone; however, I was very perseverant. I never lost focus of my goals, and always remembered how lucky I was to have a chance. No matter how difficult and hard life was at times, I was determined to conquer the impossible.

I have always worked in hotels: I started as a housekeeper, then moved on to the front desk, serving tables, and even tried my hand at cooking. I had my share of hunger and challenges, but I still managed to graduate.

No one in my family could afford to come to my graduation from Venezuela, but within three years, I became a general manager, and right away, I brought my parents to visit. Later, I brought my youngest sister after she finished high school, to study. Now, she is a professor at the University of North Texas, "Dr. Ceballos." She is the first in my family to have a PhD.

Today, I am vice president of housekeeping for over two hundred hotels, Motel 6 and Studio 6, and an executive international professional coach. I have been recognized for my leadership abilities and adaptability.

But my greatest pride is that we were able to bring my parents to live here legally in 2019, away from the dictatorship in our country. I have learned that I am a humble but unapologetically courageous leader… and that I am enough.

The pandemic of 2020 helped reinforce my belief that you always need to be prepared for change and that life is too short. Therefore, I choose to live with purpose, and help others to see that being courageous, authentic, and perseverant is the only way to live.

I always knew I would marry a woman. Fifteen years ago, I met my wife. She is a lawyer, and we have a beautiful thirteen-year-old daughter. At my "legal" wedding, in 2014, my eighty-year-old father walked me down the aisle.

I have not stopped learning and growing, because the only limitations are what I allow into my thoughts. I believe in paying forward by working with National Charity Leagues to teach my daughter the value of giving back. I am also involved with Hispanic organizations that focus on helping to develop Hispanic leaders, like Southern Methodist University (SMU) and their executive program, to develop Hispanic leaders and organizations that support coaching of youth and professionals to realize that we, Hispanics, are awesome. After all, we bring great values, we are bilingual, we are courageous, we are the future.

My values, integrity, respect, and authenticity have been the byproduct of my toughest experiences, teaching me never to be afraid of ridicule, rejection, or failure. Once you learn that those are just lessons and you are enough, there is no stopping you!

BIOGRAPHY

Lisbeth Ceballos is the vice president of housekeeping operation support at G6 Hospitality, the parent company of the iconic Motel 6 brand, and is an executive self-proclaimed agent of change.

Born in Venezuela, after graduating high school, Lisbeth left her home to pursue her dream of studying English and hospitality management. With more than two decades of leadership experience in the lodging industry, Lisbeth approaches workplace culture and leadership with a multicultural perspective. Throughout her career she has focused on self-growth and earned multiple certifications in Leadership, Strategic HR professional (SHRM-SCP), and as a leadership coach (PCC-ICF).

ASSIMILATION AND BELONGING

RAMONA CHAVEZ

"While striving so hard to assimilate, I had neglected acculturation, which is the blending of cultures."

Assimilate. This is the word that I heard all my life while living in the USA. I embraced it and attempted to be part of the circle however I could.

You see, my parents made one the most important decisions of my life that has blessed me beyond what I had even imagined. I was five years old when my father sold our home in Mexico and bought one in El Paso, TX. As a young teacher himself, he accepted that his home country was not making the best decisions based on the needs of its citizens. It was not easy, even if the move was within twenty miles. His plan was simply that his children would enroll in the school system that would allow my siblings and me an opportunity of a lifetime.

Thankfully, my grandfather had come to the US with a Bracero Worker's Visa in the sixties. It opened the door for the rest of his children to have a better life. My mother was one of twelve children that could apply for residence in the US.

Initially, I had to attend ESL classes, where I was taken out of my regular class lessons. But by the second grade, I was officially allowed to remain in the classroom on a daily basis without anyone noticing I was different. By the time I got to high school, my Spanish accent was well-avoided. After all, my skin color was just as light as some of my white friends. I dressed the part and followed the crowd to be American.

Then, it was time to apply for colleges. Unfortunately, I could not apply for most scholarships because I was not a US citizen. That's when it hit me: It wasn't just good enough to have good grades and apply for a scholarship. I couldn't just act the part, I also had to be the part.

So, I started the undertaking of getting my US citizenship at eighteen. It included a hefty fee with a long waiting period. After the help of my older sister to fill out the meticulously long application, several loans to pay for my college, many part-time jobs, a name change due to marriage, and finally completing my Bachelor of Science after five years, I was a true United States Citizen.

However, people continuously asking me in my home state of Texas where I was from made me feel as if I didn't belong. While being a citizen, I thought for sure I would belong by having an education, being economically stable, and having American friends, but it was not enough. Maybe I would never be the American citizen they envisioned.

Therefore, I began the journey of finding who I was truly

meant to be. My father had always reminded me that these lands were inhabited by my ancestors before the Europeans. I learned the importance of acculturation over assimilation. While striving so hard to assimilate, I had neglected acculturation, which is the blending of cultures.

Now, as I send my older sons to college, I encourage them to belong as they are and pridefully embody real citizenship. I remind them that our ancestors from these lands continue to live through us. I pride myself in feeling the satisfaction of raising world citizens and not religious souls.

BIOGRAPHY

Ramona Chavez is a sociologist, community advocate, volunteer, entrepreneur, world traveler, and blogger of Mona's Family Emporium. Her latest projects include celebrations around the world and ethnography (the study of customs and cultures).

Ramona has lived/traveled across the globe and loves to share her experience surrounding cultural competency and awareness. She enjoys writing and has published articles in *Living Magazine, Southlake Style Magazine,* and Gateway People's social media relating to "Gathering at the Table."

Ramona was born in Mexico, migrated to the United States at the age of five, and submitted her naturalized citizen documents upon entering college in hopes of receiving a scholarship, but it was not finalized until after she completed her bachelor's degree.

MANUELITA CODY

"Life will present you with unthinkable challenges. We must adapt and pivot to learning, growing, and blossoming."

The world has changed. After experiencing the pandemic, we are different. Our priorities are different, as are our goals and the way we work. We communicate differently; our relationships have changed. If we learned anything, it is that life will present you with unthinkable challenges and that we must adapt and pivot to learn, grow, and blossom.

One of my life's missions has been to never stop learning. I applied it as a student. I applied it when I moved from Colombia to the United States and learned a new language and culture. I applied it when I became a parent. I apply it every day if I can.

I applied it to my story, which I now share: I had been working in the financial industry for over fifteen years and felt ready to do something new. Someone approached me with an opportunity with a foreign company in a completely different field: mining and steel production. *Why not?*

I had worked for them out of college as an intern and they remembered me. I was hired to be their treasurer. I had to learn on the job, but I made that leap! It was a difficult transition.

It was a different industry and different work culture from what I was used to, and even though I spoke Spanish, I felt out of place.

But slowly, I grew more at ease. I was being groomed to do every job at that office, and I embraced it. After all, my mission has always been to never stop learning. After only two years, everything changed again. The president at headquarters in Chile passed away and that meant structural changes, mainly for the New York office. Was leaving the financial industry a mistake? I could lose my job. I was the least senior person. To my dismay, I was the only one left standing. I survived the brutal layoffs and was now in charge of the whole operation. As someone working in public affairs and legal representation, I learned my new job again.

My biggest growth as a professional was around the corner. As the "face" of this international company in the United States, it meant exactly that. I was the contact and the promoter of its good will. And under my leadership, we joined the Chilean Chamber of Commerce in New York.

Soon after, the Board of Directors invited me to join them. That was a giant leap. I had no experience being part of a board. It was time to learn new things again. I became a very active contributing board member.

After five years, it was time to re-elect a new president of the chamber, and to my surprise, all eyes turned to me. I was their candidate of choice. I was the first female president in an over-100-year-history of this organization. I have been president of the North American Chilean Chamber of Commerce for five years, and it is the work I have cherished the most. I know other opportunities will present themselves. I must be open to them and be willing to NEVER STOP LEARNING.

BIOGRAPHY

Manuelita Cody was born in Cali-Colombia and grew up in Bogotá. She attended Gimnasio Femenino, an all-girls Catholic school. Forced to leave Colombia at the age of sixteen due to its social instability, Manuelita moved to the United States, where she learned English and eventually graduated cum laude from Adelphi University in Garden City, NY with a Bachelor's in Business Administration.

Manuelita worked in the financial services industry for many years as a financial advisor, trainer and supervisor. She transitioned to a different industry and career and has been the president of the North American Chilean Chamber of Commerce since 2016.

FEAR IS THE BIGGEST OBSTACLE FOR ANY HUMAN BEING

SHARIMAR COLÓN-RODRÍGUEZ

"Fear is the biggest obstacle for any human being. I knew I needed to overcome my fears—I was not being myself."

My story and life begin in Aibonito, a small town in the middle of the mountains located in the center of Puerto Rico. I grew up close to my parents and siblings in a neighborhood where everybody knew each other. Doors were never locked; neighbors would come to the house like they were part of the family or would come by just to have a cup of coffee. My experience growing up in this environment has made me a person that values family and community above all else.

A proud product of the public school system, I was accepted into the electrical engineering program at the University of Puerto Rico, and I moved to the west side of the island to pursue my studies. It was the first time I moved away from home and my small town. Right before I graduated, I was recruited to work in a nuclear plant in Alabama. At the age of twenty-three, I left behind my entire family and my island and moved to the mainland with only two suitcases of clothes.

I received a big dose of culture shock when I got to the United States. I lived in the same apartment for six years, but never met my neighbors. This was a far cry from what I was used to. My family was constantly getting together with food and music when I was growing up, but here in the States, I did not have a family. I felt like I did not belong to this place. I wanted to pack everything again and go back home, but I knew my future was here in the US.

My English vocabulary was very limited, and I was only able to answer with my head—nodding for yes and shaking my head for no—because of the fear I had of making mistakes and saying nonsensical things. I was always known as an extrovert and a leader in school and in the community in PR, but the frustration of an unknown culture and language was holding me back, personally and professionally. It was just fear manifesting.

Fear is the biggest obstacle for any human being. I knew I needed to overcome my fears —I was not being myself. My responsibilities as a nuclear professional, the opportunities given to me by Southern Nuclear, and my involvement in my community have helped me move on from my fears. Nowadays, I have been recognized for my leadership skills and have held positions in different departments within my company where I have had the opportunity to have a positive impact on society and make a difference.

BIOGRAPHY

Sharimar Colón-Rodríguez is an electrical engineer from Aibonito, Puerto Rico, currently working as a design engineer with Southern Nuclear in Alabama. She graduated magna cum laude in 2013 and was selected to be part of several recognized groups such as the Tau Beta Pi Honor Society, Fem Prof, and has received multiple scholarships for her leadership and honors.

As part of her current design role, she is responsible for design development and equipment for commercial nuclear plants. She also serves as a leader in different groups, including being the current chair of the Diversity, Equity, and Inclusion council for her facility.

PATRICIA CONDE-BROOKS

"Educados y preparados, we want to open doors and opportunities for others."

This story shares the path to education and preparation for my brother Dr. Richard Conde, PhD, and myself. We immigrated from Colombia in 1975 and settled in Earlsboro, Oklahoma, a rural town of 800 people, where we were the only Latino family.

Growing up in Oklahoma, my mother believed it was important to continue our Colombian culture, which entailed eating the same food, listening to our beloved cumbias, and maintaining communication in the Spanish language within the family, to keep ties to our origins and our extended family.

While our mother could not always help us with our studies, she instilled in us a work ethic, held high expectations for us, and was largely supportive. Our teachers and counselors, though well-intentioned, always made us feel uncomfortable when congratulating us for our ability to speak articulately—or for any achievement, really—as if intelligence and fortitude were impossible for young Latino immigrants. Through resiliency and *pa'lante* tenacity, we became first-generation college graduates.

As Latinos living in the United States, we have always felt a sense of responsibility to others in underrepresented and marginalized groups. As students, we rarely had the opportunity to interact with teachers or administrators who could serve as role models for us. Sadly, our professional experiences showed us that Latinos are often not represented at the table and their voices are not heard. But we wanted to find a way to both educate and prepare the next generation of Latinos. We knew that education both opens doors and changes lives. It was this desire to make a difference and our Latino *pa'lante* spirit that had us pursuing doctorate degrees in our fifties.

By all accounts, the odds of a Latino obtaining a doctoral degree are very low. Most of us have to overcome obstacles to a new language, new culture, poverty, uneducated parents, unsupportive parents, low-income *barrios* (neighborhoods), and first-generation status. Latinos have the lowest percentage of graduate degrees compared to all other non-Hispanics.

Our resilience was our driving force: We were constantly having to prove that low-income immigrants like us deserved a place in higher education. On our journey, we encountered racial/ethnic stereotyping and low expectations of our abilities. Our *conocimientos* of resistance and survival—handed down, consciously and unconsciously, by *la familia*—offered support that helped us arrive at where we are today. It's in our fifties that we have found our sense of purpose as educators. We have become part of the 0.2% of Latinos who hold a doctorate degree. As Latino educators, we serve as positive, professional role models for the students with whom we work. Working in higher education, we have been able to open doors of communication with our community, given our shared language and cultural background. Dr. Richard Conde is a professor at a Hispanic serving institution. I work within higher education in helping students overcome the systemic barriers that limit the success of marginalized populations. *Educados y preparados*, we want to open doors and opportunities for others.

BIOGRAPHY

Dr. Patricia Conde-Brookes is a higher education and organizational development professional with extensive experience working with diverse groups and organizations to increase individual and collective effectiveness and inclusion. Her organizational development focus is on the simultaneity of race, ethnicity, gender, and class, and the opportunities and challenges these differences create in organizations. Her academic research focuses on career and leadership development for Latinas and women of color in organizations.

MY RECIPE OF POWER

SOFIA CORCHO

"Never break the promises you made to yourself. Remember that you are your most powerful resource to accomplish everything you aim for."

In trying to find an interesting story to share in this book, the only recurrent theme that I found was how when I fall, I stand up as quickly as possible. Lately, when I fall, I don't feel pain anymore; I liken it to training for a marathon and embracing the suck. I even laugh about it, especially when I fall with style only to get back up as if nothing happened. The important point here is that I can make fun of myself; I am kind and positive in my inner talks, and I have come to terms with the fact that nothing is perfect or permanent. Life is full of imperfections, and nothing lasts forever—even the rough patches will disappear at some point.

To illustrate this, I can share with you some of my most pivotal moments, like the time I organized a $100 US raffle to buy my flight ticket to America and arrived here with $20 US in my pocket; when I worked as a teacher without knowing English; or the time I became a victim of domestic violence and chose to be my own lawyer and read my victim impact statement with my broken English in front of a room full of male strangers. These struggles, or "falls" molded me into the woman I am today—and taught me to get up that much faster each time.

I can also share the happiest moments of my life, like when I became a first-generation graduate student and paid for my student debt with my second business in the United States; also, the joy I have every time I help other Latinas to fight for their fair share or when I support Latino founders to scale their business in the United States.

I have so many fantastic memories to share, like when I traveled for free for a year and got to explore forty out of the fifty-one states, spent three months in Puerto Rico teaching myself how to swim, and went to Hawaii and spotted my first whale, but my wish for you is to have my recipe of power, the one that has gotten me so far, made me so happy and so much stronger.

This is my secret to overcoming the most difficult moments—and it's helped me do more than just survive; it's helped me thrive.

1. Stick to your purpose and never forget why you are in this world. It is crucial that you know what your true calling is.

2. Be your own biggest cheerleader and advocate, always believe in your potential, and stay away from the noise of people who didn't accomplish their dreams.

3. Never break the promises you made to yourself; remember that you are your most powerful resource to accomplish everything you aim for.

If you keep these three things very close to your heart every day, no matter how painful, sad, or unfair things can become for you, remember: everything will eventually pass. Life isn't perfect, but you can count on your positive and strong spirit to continue your journey. Always play your music and defend your sacred priorities. The people that belong to your circle will dance with you, support your efforts, and respect your boundaries. Be a proud Latina and don't be afraid of showing your authentic self in America. Be #sinpena with a big smile, because nothing is perfect or permanent in this life and everything should pass, but your smile is what people will always remember about you!

BIOGRAPHY

Sofia Corcho is an early-stage startup consultant and advisor with a focus on digital solutions and international startups. She is currently a managing partner of AccelHUB Venture Partners, ScaleUp LatAm, and Accelerate Italy. She is passionate about entre-leadership, innovation, and social impact.

Sofia is a proud first-generation graduate student with an MBA from Cambridge College. With a background in building and leading implementation, product consulting, and operations teams, Sofia has extensive experience in creating internal positions and processes, managing client project implementations, and developing client relationships. She has over ten years of business-to-business relationship management, operations leadership, and product consulting in consumer goods and technology start-ups.

VICKY COVARRUBIAS

"Education is the passport to the future, for tomorrow belongs to those who prepare for it today."

I am a Latina born in Zacatecas, Mexico. I lived with my parents until I was sixteen, when I decided to move to the city to live with my aunt and study. I always loved studying, and in the little *ranchito,* we didn't have many opportunities.

When I was in middle school, I used to walk about five kilometers every day with friends just to go to school. I studied accounting, and after I graduated, I went to live with my sister in Guadalajara, Mexico to find work.

When I was twenty years old, I came to US to visit my brothers and I loved it here. I saw a lot of opportunities and decided to stay. It was so hard at the beginning, because I did not speak the language and I did not have a green card; I had only a visa.

I then met my husband and got married. I always wanted to continue studying, and attended night classes after I got married, receiving my high school diploma in six months. All this while I was eight months pregnant, expecting my first child. I have always believed in myself and what I can accomplish.

While taking care of my first son full-time, I was presented with the opportunity to receive my green card. That is when I started pursuing my dreams. I went to college and I had two little ones; by that time my son was four and my daughter was three. I wanted to find something I could do while still taking care of them. I decided to get into real estate and passed my state exam on the first try. I have been in real estate helping families achieve the "American Dream" since 2007. It is a total honor for me to be part of their journey and guide them, and my most important reward is seeing their faces when I hand them the keys to their new home.

Real estate has taught me a lot. I have grown so much as a person, and I still love to learn by reading personal development books. This profession is sometimes challenging, like many others, but for me what helps me overcome any obstacles is self-care. I am a marathon runner; I love to run, and it has taught me a lot of lessons. I am currently on pace to run 1,000+ miles in 2021.

Above all, I am a very persistent person. My main goal is to set a good example and be a good influence for my kids, so they can achieve whatever they want to in life—and the first step for them is to get an education.

I never thought that the little girl that used to walk five kilometers to school each day could one day be helping families with probably the biggest investment of their lives: to own a home.

BIOGRAPHY

Vicky Covarrubias was born in Zacatecas, Mexico, and came to the United States at the age of twenty. She currently resides in Los Angeles, CA, with her husband of twenty-five years and four kids.

She is a professional real estate agent that specializes in residential real estate and has been in business for over fourteen years helping families become homeowners. Her most important goal in life is to leave her kids a legacy of EXCELLENCE, honesty, and service to others. She loves to spend time with her family and her hobbies are reading, hiking, and running.

CURIOSITY AND LEARNING CAN TAKE YOU ANYWHERE

ILIANA CRUZ

"My answer was always the same: be genuinely curious and eager to learn."

I landed at Miami International Airport in 2010, five months pregnant, having left all my family behind except for my husband. This transition was extremely challenging, becoming a mother while leaving mine behind in Mexico. I also knew that it would be so much more difficult to pass on family history and Latin customs to my baby, when it depended only on me.

This change, however, did not come as a surprise. From an early age, I was interested in learning about languages and different cultures and understanding how people in other countries live and thrive.

After high school, I spent one summer in Canada. I didn't know it then, but that trip turned out to be the event that changed my life. In Canada, I met my husband and became fluent in English, which opened the door to Miami.

Miami became my home. It allowed me to stay connected to my language, Spanish, and I was surrounded by Latin culture. I was thriving in a logistics career, in charge of sixteen countries, and frequently flying within the US, Latin America, and Europe. During this time, the question people asked me the most was: how did I do it? My team members in other countries wanted to learn the steps I took to get promoted, get transferred, and get a job like mine. My answer was always the same: be genuinely curious and eager to learn. Curiosity will make you question the status quo, find new things, and challenge existing paradigms. Learning will help you understand how things work.

I realized I loved teaching others what I knew. I took advantage of every opportunity to give training online or in person. Even on my last day in logistics, I hosted an online training that went live in every one of our offices around the globe.

Now, flying solo, that is what I do. I teach others what I have learned after two decades of working in a corporate environment. I do this because I believe a person that is happy and productive in their job will start spreading a wave of positivity all around.

My family in Mexico taught me the value of hard work. My children showed me the importance of being a good example. Every person I have worked with has left something in me that keeps pushing me to help others become fantastic, energetic, and driven leaders.

After so many years of being away from childhood home, I still miss my family every day. I have learned, however, how to make each new city my new home and find beauty everywhere I go.

Can anyone overcome challenges and achieve goals? I believe yes, we can. We all have the opportunity to be a little bit better today than yesterday. We all can learn and improve anything. We can achieve any goal. Every step counts!

BIOGRAPHY

Iliana Cruz is a leadership coach with clients on three continents. She graduated with honors with a Bachelor's degree in International Business Administration, which launched her career in logistics.

She has lived in four different countries and learned about the cultures and how other people rate success. A mother of two children, she values flexibility and time-saving hacks. For this purpose, she has decided to work exclusively online, allowing her to take clients from anywhere in the world and make her own schedule. She bases her method on four pillars: time management, productive habits, workplace boundaries, and leadership skills.

EXACTLY WHERE I'M SUPPOSED TO BE

ADRIANA DAVIES

"Challenges are what make life interesting. Overcoming them is what makes life meaningful."

My mother and grandmother instilled the core value of determination in me. In 1907, my grandmother became a young widow and moved her family to the US in search of opportunity and safety. I think of the strength it took for her to make that trip alone to a foreign country with five children, more than a hundred years ago. Like her, I've never let the fear of failing stop me from pursuing my dreams.

Since emigrating from Bogotá, Colombia to the US, my journey's been a *pulso* with experiences that made me strong, confident, and successful. Everyone faces challenges, and, while it may not feel like it at the time, they aren't negative; they're necessary for growth.

My experiences as an immigrant make me resourceful. I can create opportunities for myself—and my community and the companies where I've worked. I had a successful career in Colombia when I moved to the US twenty-four years ago, but my experience wasn't valid here. So, I started over as a waitress. While I earned my living serving meals, I assessed my skills and how to build on them to succeed in a new country and culture.

After seven months of applying to corporate jobs without an interview, I found my first role at Honeywell. I never saw my potential as limited. I went on to earn two more degrees including a master's in law, international compliance, and risk management.

The hardest work started when my daughter got sick at nine years old. Soon after I had my first director role, she was diagnosed with ulcerative colitis. This obstacle put me at odds with my career progression. I struggled to figure out where I belonged—at home or leading in the workplace and maintaining my role as my family's breadwinner. I broke through stereotypes of what I thought it meant to be a mother, a role model, and a Latina.

Today, I'm a senior director of compliance at Medtronic—and my daughter is happy and healthy, pursuing her post-secondary education. I ensure my business complies with regulatory and legal requirements and policies.

When I was growing up, my mother involved me in social projects with patients, single moms, and people of need. She never let anything stop her. Like my mother, I get energized by fixing things that benefit the greater good, like compliance.

I've "fixed" my perceived weaknesses and turned them into strengths. I used to be insecure because my English wasn't always as good as my colleagues. But my accent and English skills aren't obstacles; it just means I approach situations differently, and I'm a better listener and communicator for it.

From the start, I've worked hard, stayed flexible, and reinvented myself. No experience, positive or negative, goes to waste. At every step, I've found an ally, teacher, or friend to help further my progress. My journey is far from complete, and I can't say what obstacles I may face next, but I know I'll overcome them and find myself exactly where I'm supposed to be.

BIOGRAPHY

Adriana Davies is the senior director of compliance of Medtronic, with a proven track record of best-in-class programmatic solutions that reshape and nurture culture of diversity and minimize legal risk.

Adriana is a Colombian emigree who earned a Master's in Law, focusing on International Compliance & Risk Management, magna cum laude, from Thomas Jefferson School of Law. She also holds a BS in business administration, magna cum laude, from North Carolina Wesleyan College, as well as certifications in D&I from Cornell University, healthcare compliance from Seton Hall University, and she is a CCEP Certified Ethics & Compliance Professional.

RAFAEL H. DE ANDA

"Life isn't complicated, especially with a taco in your hand."

I thought to myself, "From today on, my life will be different." I boarded a bus in a strange land with the name of a saint, San Diego, knowing it wasn't anything like my hometown of Arandas, Jalisco. My friend ran up to me and gave me a sweet tasting *torta* that I couldn't finish. It had a type of salsa that was red and sweet instead of spicy. No doubt it would be years before I would be back among the agave fields in my hometown. The one message that ran through my mind was, "I made it." Once I arrived at my destination in Orange County, California, to be with my family, I knew that was where the real work would begin.

I started work the following week picking cabbages. The days were long and the work was tough, but I would not have had it any other way. I had made more money in that first week than I ever made making sandals and selling candy on the streets of Jalisco. After work, tacos were always on the menu. Nothing else could connect me back to my roots like tacos. We would jokingly call it "the Mexican hamburger." The only thing missing was the flavor. It never tasted quite right.

We scraped together our savings and, together with my family, we started selling tacos out of a food truck. The nights were grueling and long. I would carry a pistol with me to protect myself in the event any of our "friends" wanted to take my only opportunity at my "American Dream."

We would drive to the LA farmer's market at dawn in order to be ready by noon to serve until 3 a.m. when the bars closed. Making everything by hand was the way to go. From chopping the *asada* and the *cabesa* to prepping the *horchata*, the flavors had to be just right.

After a couple years, we saved enough money to purchase our first location in 1980. The same thought ran through my head: I had made it.

I always struggled in school, since it was always taught in another language, English. I was, however, familiar with tacos, expanding my knowledge in an area that I knew would benefit me. Over the course of the next twenty years, the love for my heritage spurred me to open more than ten locations all over Orange County, CA.

Today, my work is different, as I have the privilege to work with my two sons, Raphael and Christian, who both share the same love for their roots as I do. They have the same drive and determination that helped me push through adversity; I see it in them. Together we operate Taqueria Hoy and 4 Copas Organic Tequila.

The "American Dream" did not come easy for me, but I wouldn't have it any other way. My goal is to inspire the next generation of Mexican Americans through my story to work hard, never give up, and always live every day like it could be their last.

BIOGRAPHY

Rafael H. De Anda comes from Arandas, Jalisco, and is the owner of Taqueria Hoy and 4 Copas Organic Tequila. His elder son Raphael completed his BA at Chapman University and his MBA at I.E. Business School in Madrid, Spain. His younger son Christian completed his BS at Chapman University.

The family has served on the boards of various nonprofit organizations, such as the Associates Board of the Second Harvest Food Bank Orange County, TECMA Orange County, and the CHOC Hospital Latino Advisory Council.

RIMA DE BIEN

"What is your legacy?"

In the 1950s, my grandparents made the tough decision to leave Puerto Rico and seek a better life in the United States. It was especially difficult for my father to be transported from the lush tropics to the concrete jungle.

My father tried to adapt to New York City, but in *el barrio,* prejudice was pervasive. To avoid a gang of name-calling Italians seeking retribution, he would jump from rooftop to rooftop in narrow escape of their wrath.

Inauspiciously, at school my father encountered similar prejudice, but more demeaning in nature. In a dank classroom, my father stared at words on a blackboard as foreign as Egyptian hieroglyphics. When he asked a Spanish-speaking student a question, Mrs. Berg reprimanded them viciously: "No speaking Spanish in school," to which they simply nodded. She then threw her hands up in exasperation and tapped her temples to signify to the class they were idiots. At her mockery, the class burst into raucous laughter. From that moment on, school became an ordeal my father was forced to endure.

Placed in "special needs" classes, my father and other Spanish-speaking students were ostracized, bullied, and labeled "retarded" by white classmates, as teachers often purported the same sentiment. Consequently, my father found little resolve to strive academically in fear of humiliation.

To make matters worse, unexpectedly his father died. My father was only fifteen.

Fatherless, my father felt a responsibility to make something out of himself in gratitude for his father's efforts. All the bias, all the abuse, and all the hatred made my father study more. With fortitude, he became the first person in our family to graduate college, whereby he became a teacher. He taught the supposed, "unteachable," and changed young lives as a result.

Regrettably, when he had us, he made us "assimilate" by only speaking English to avoid prejudice. In his mind he was doing us a favor, but really, he finished the job those teachers started on him.

I believe there are consequences when you abandon meaningful, impactful traditions of your culture, like a language. Statistics indicate that in 2030, half the world will be speaking Spanish. Therefore, it's a shame to abandon a custom like: *"Bendición,"* meaning, "bless me," that is answered with, *"Dios te bendiga"* meaning, "God bless you." Even today, most Hispanic households use this blessing before a loved one departs.

Luckily, as prejudice diminishes and inclusion takes its place,

I know I have a choice. I can celebrate my ancestors' traditions, heritage, and culture. I can learn Spanish and ask my father for his blessing and appreciate the response. I can stand for diversity, equality, and inclusion, because our lives are a culmination of what we stand for.

What do you stand for? I invite you to stand up and be counted by representing your Latin culture. That's why I do things like become an ambassador for *Hispanic Star*, because we all have a choice.

BIOGRAPHY

Rima De Bien is a producer who produces tough stories about human trafficking, domestic violence, and child abuse. As an actor, she has done primarily commercial work but can be seen on *FBI,* and *Russian Doll* this season.

Rima serves as board liaison for New York Women in Film and Television and is a board member of Women in the Arts and Media Coalition. She is also on the SAG-AFTRA Women's Diversity Committee. Rima is currently writing a non-fictional musical about her life as a runaway. She attended LaGuardia High School for the Performing Arts, Carnegie Mellon University, and holds a BA.

TAKE THE DETOUR

JOSÉ DE JESÚS

"I knew my life would change, but I figured this was just a detour."

We all knew the drill. If it was Saturday, my siblings and I would soon be piling into the car with my dad at the wheel and my mom in the passenger seat. On her lap, a foil-wrapped dish of arroz con *gandules;* the aroma of cilantro, onions, and peppers would fill the car, even with the windows down. We would make the drive from our home in Guaynabo on the northern coast of Puerto Rico up to the mountains to spend the day with family in Barranquitas.

I loved *sábados.* For me, this magical day was filled with family, friends, or, my personal favorite: crispy-skinned roasted pig. It was a tradition. The cousins played in the yard, the adults played dominos, and we all got our chance to turn the pig as it roasted over the pit. It's no wonder that I fell in love with pork, as most Hispanics do, but my affinity went beyond the norm.

When I left my island home to attend college—in Iowa—I

knew my life would change, but I figured this was just a detour, and I'd return after graduation. (When people ask why I chose to go to Iowa, I tell them I got a surfing scholarship, but it was actually volleyball!)

While I was pursuing a communications degree, I was also in constant pursuit of keeping my family traditions alive. My parents would send care packages filled with the flavors of home like Adobo and Sazón, and I would put them to good use, introducing my college friends to delicious Latin dishes. One of those friends was a beautiful Iowan girl who grew up in Dyersville, the location for the movie *Field of Dreams*. Six years later, she became my wife, the eventual mother of our two children, and an honorary *Boricua*.

In 2013, I landed a job with the National Pork Board. For a Puerto Rican who eats, sleeps, and breathes pork, it was a dream job—and still is. The late Steve Jobs said, "The only way to do great work is to love what you do." I get to share my love of pork with people and help the pork industry understand the business opportunity that exists today with multicultural consumers. With sixty-three million Hispanics in the US and growing, we are pork's future, and I'm excited to be a part of it.

Over the years, my brother, sister, and parents all moved to the Hawkeye State, and we take turns hosting our family gatherings, where pork is always on the table. Even on New Year's Eve, when the wind chill is twenty degrees below zero and I'm outside roasting a pig in *La Caja China*, I am grateful that my Midwest detour turned out to be so much more.

BIOGRAPHY

José de Jesús is the senior director of multicultural marketing with the National Pork Board in Des Moines, Iowa. He earned his BA in communications at Clarke University, Iowa, and his MPA at Bellevue University, Nebraska.

Previously, he was an award-winning journalist who covered government, cultural affairs, and other topics for newspapers in Iowa and Wisconsin. In 2020, José was named Marketer of the Year by the Iowa American Marketing Association. His Instagram account (@lechonasado) is used to promote pork dishes, develop relationships within the food industry, and raise awareness of pork's versatility.

THE POWER OF CELEBRATIONS,
"WHAT IF?" AND "WHY NOT?"

DR. AMPARO DE LA PEÑA

"A series of unexpected celebrations, "what ifs" and "why nots" have guided my life and career."

Growing up in the eighties (the 1980s, that is), students in Uruguay had to choose in ninth grade between pursuing a career in the sciences or the humanities. As a daughter of two literature teachers, and being a voracious bookworm, I had been nevertheless fascinated by the natural sciences from an early age and had spent my summers studying all kinds of bugs, crabs and frogs. To their surprise (my parents', not the bugs), I enrolled in the Chemistry College.

In 1984, this was the most difficult college and coursework in the country; in my mother's words, it was character-forming. Exams were designed to be failed repeatedly, and the system was geared to filter out those that were not hard-headed or high-spirited enough to keep trying. The first three years (which took about six in real life) were focused on several levels of chemistry, physics, and mathematics. Up until then, I had yet to find my true professional passion.

What kept me going was a resilience borne out of having lived through a dictatorship and having seen (in disbelief) how my parents defiantly celebrated, after being forcefully removed from their jobs. We lived paycheck to paycheck, and it was the end of the month. Having spent the last money they had on a few roses, a champagne bottle, and some provolone, their life lesson was to ask, "Why not?"

They said: "Why not celebrate? Today, we are alive and together. Our livelihood, our home, even our lives can be taken away, but not our spirit. So today, we celebrate! Tomorrow, we'll figure it out." And so they did, and so did I, as I continued on with the second part of the curriculum, which consisted of applied sciences.

One day, I listened to a talk about a new drug-monitoring unit at the University Hospital, where the doses of medication patients were given were individualized according to their blood values. "What if I volunteered?" I thought. And after about a year of volunteering, I met a kind professor who encouraged me to apply to the graduate program in pharmaceutics at the University of Florida. "Why not?" I said. He would later teach me to turn perceived challenges into opportunities, and he celebrated every one of his students' accomplishments.

In essence, a series of unexpected celebrations, "what ifs" and "why nots" have guided my life and career. I celebrated an invitation from University of Florida, a cancer diagnosis, and a business "mistake" that turned into an opportunity. And I said "why not?" to an offer to join Eli Lilly, when asked to lead a COVID team in 2020, and then offered to write this part of my story. And I said "what if?", when invited to write about cancer, and about love, and when offered to switch professional roles

I'd like to propose this to you: every time a challenge looks scary, or even impossible, try celebrating first, and then asking: "why not?" and "what if?" You just may be surprised.

BIOGRAPHY

Dr. Amparo de la Peña is an inspirational leader, a mother, scientist, and writer. She earned a degree in pharmaceutical chemistry from the University of the Republic, Uruguay, and a PhD in Pharmaceutics from the University of Florida. In more than twenty-one years at Eli Lilly, where she leads cross-functional drug development teams, her scientific expertise has helped bring drugs to patients worldwide.

Dr. de la Peña has written for over 130 scientific publications and is involved with scientific associations. She is a proud mother of three energetic teenagers and writes short nonfiction stories in her free time. Dr. de la Peña is a board member of the Indianapolis Public Library Foundation; her passion is increasing the diversity of the readership and library materials.

THE JOURNEY TO FINDING MY POWER

PATRICIA DIAZ

"I was tired of feeling powerless and, in the process, I found myself and my purpose."

Sometimes, you find yourself surrounded by a sea of people and you get swallowed in it. You stick out like a sore thumb, but you do your best to blend in, to not draw any more attention to yourself. Swimming with the current is easier than swimming against it. But once it spits you back out, you don't recognize the version that is in front of the mirror. That's how immigration felt for me. I lost myself and the spark that made me one in a billion, but I don't blame myself.

Growing up in a predominantly white state after moving to the United States at the age of nine, I often found myself searching with no luck for others who resembled me. I wondered where I belonged while doing my best to fit in. In high school I finally found other Latinos. The joy and sense of relief I felt left as quickly as it came, though. According to them, I was whitewashed.

Have you ever felt not "Latina enough"?

My mom would cook Peruvian dishes at home, but I sometimes preferred a burger. Did that make me not "Latina enough"? I have more knowledge of the US government and history than I do of my home country. We would put an American flag outside our home every Fourth of July. Did that make me not "Latina enough"? It's like battling which side of you to choose.

After winning a scholarship for Latinos, I felt like a fraud. I could no longer hide this struggle within me, the weight too much to bear, yet it was difficult to express. Did others also notice I had lost my *Latinidad*? But how can you mourn a version of yourself that you never met? You cannot lose something you never had. You cannot embrace something you never had a hold of.

I am not from here nor there. There is no battle to be fought, no side to choose. I could also no longer hide the parts that made me *me*, and that is my *Latinidad*. I needed to learn about my culture, food, ancestors, and history. I learned to honor both cultures with pride. Once I owned that, I set myself free.

I was tired of feeling powerless and in the process, I found myself and my purpose. I want to help other Latinos in this country embrace their story and, in turn, find their power. There is power in owning your story; you can own it, or it can own you.

For those struggling to do so, my advice is: We can only do what's best for us. There's no right or wrong way to be Latina/o, but it is wrong to shame others into thinking they're not if they don't act, behave, or think the way you think a Latino should. The definition of Latina is personal. Be kind to others; we are all struggling to find our place and space in this country.

BIOGRAPHY

Patricia Diaz has a BS in finance and economics, and a MS in finance. After struggling to find her voice as a Latina in the United States, she founded Latinos Empowered—an online platform dedicated to empowering Latinos in the US by providing information and resources on finance, career, and health. Their mission is for Latinos to understand their potential and power in this country by providing guidance and tools that drive action and conversation in the Latinx community.

Patricia is hopeful that this Latinx generation can change the current narrative and take back their power.

GILDA DORIA

"Decide exactly what you want for your life and let go of everything that distracts you, stops you, and holds you back from creating what you deserve."

If you asked me when I was five years old what I wanted to be when I grew up, the answer, without hesitation, would've been professional soccer player. My ultimate dream was to play in the Olympics or World Cup for the United States or Paraguay.

There are many big decisions in life—who you marry, your first home purchase, how you raise your kids, and where you decide to go to college or educate yourself. When making these types of decisions, for the most part, you spend a lot of time thinking it over and discussing it with trusted friends and family, seeking their support and guidance.

My college decision process was a big one for me. As an elite athlete, I spent hundreds of hours on the soccer field, practicing and perfecting my game in order to play at the highest level. I had big expectations for my playing career, as well as the doors and opportunities that soccer could open for me. I was looking at various Division 1 scholarship offers to play soccer at the highest level. The only problem was that my dream school was Duke University, and that was one of the colleges that was not as interested in me during the recruitment process.

My coaches, support system, and friends encouraged me to pursue other scholarship opportunities and go after the safer options, where I knew I could get a good education and be valued on the field. This made me really discouraged, and the lack of support made me uneasy about what I had committed I wanted to accomplish for myself—play and educate myself at Duke University.

When faced with this difficult decision, I remembered the words one of my mentors said to me: "At the end of the day, you are the one responsible for your decisions, and the one who holds the key to create with your life and what you want it to be." I was not brought into this world to live someone else's life; I was brought here to create the life I envisioned for myself. The only person who can hold me back from accomplishing my goals is myself.

One National Championship appearance, two NCAA Elite Eights, a Duke undergraduate degree, a Fuqua Business School degree, and two years of captaining Duke Women's Soccer team later, I can safely say that creating the life you want for yourself, despite what others think, is absolutely in your control. Don't let small minds tell you cannot accomplish what you want to create for your life. It is important to decide exactly what you want for your life and let go of everything that gets in your way. I learned that you need to always bet on yourself, because you are the master of your fate.

BIOGRAPHY

Gilda Doria is the ecosystem partner manager for Call for Code at IBM. She works with IBM clients on Call for Code, which invites developers and problem solvers to build and contribute to sustainable open-source software solutions that address social and humanitarian issues, while ensuring solutions are deployed to make a real difference.

Prior to her current role, Gilda served in Corporate Social Responsibility (CSR) where she brought focus in education reform, sustainability, and economic recovery to her territory. Her other experiences at IBM include more than three years in sales and one year as the chief of staff to the former IBM CIO.

Gilda holds a master's degree from Duke's Fuqua School of Business, where she was a two-time captain of the Duke's Division I Women's Soccer team.

OUR SEAT AT THE TABLE

CAROLYN DUEÑAS

"There are educated Latinas and they too can have a seat at the big table."

My mother migrated legally to Miami from Honduras, seeking a better future from what she knew. She did not have many opportunities given to her, and, like many women who migrate from Central America, she ended up working as a housekeeper.

Luckily for me, the one thing she knew to be important was an education. She worked tirelessly to send my siblings and me to a private high school. She'd drop us off and pick us up religiously, without fail. One year, I was the only one in the entire high school who had a perfect attendance. I was so proud receiving my certificate, even though everyone thought it was such a nerdy accomplishment.

Now that I'm a mother of two and learning about the educational system, I can appreciate the sacrifices she made for us. I'm even more amazed with what she was able to accomplish with her minimal resources and doing so not dominating the English language.

My mother didn't have expectations for herself, because there were none given to her. She was happy and content working hard and being able to provide for her kids. She worked for a Mexican family for many years. The eldest daughter of this family had many accolades, with an MBA and law degree being among them. She was also a CFO and VP at two big corporations. She was the most accomplished woman I knew growing up, and I'd ask myself how I could be as educated and influential as her. She gave me my first job and showed me there are educated Latinas, and they too can have a seat at the big table; Hispanics can do more than menial jobs.

I've always enjoyed taking care of people, and that is why I became a nurse. During my years as a nurse, however, I felt there was a huge disconnect between how healthcare decisions were being made and how it ultimately affected patients at their bedside. I wanted to understand the business side of healthcare, so, after seventeen years of bedside nursing and at the age of thirty-nine, with one and three-year-old children, I decided to go back to school.

I graduated in 2018 with an executive healthcare MBA from the University of Miami. One of my proudest moments was seeing my family watch me receive my diploma. My mom was able to see the fruits of her labor, as I was the first in the family to graduate with a master's.

My daughters also learned you can never stop learning. I want my daughters to know that the world we live in has its challenges, but we can overcome them with perseverance and believing enough in ourselves to not choose to be the status quo. I continue to learn how to find my seat at the table and use my voice to represent and make real change. The doors are opening, but we must knock on them!

BIOGRAPHY

Carolyn Dueñas has been a registered nurse for twenty years, with licenses in the states of California and Florida. She was an actively engaged member of several committees at BHSF. She has participated in Core Disaster Life Support through the American Medical Association. She also participated in Wave 3 of the MACRA Episode-Based Cost Measure Clinical Subcommittee.

Carolyn did a podcast on women's reproductive health on The Spicy Life Podcast on Dash Talk X. She was recently helping her community as a Case Navigator for AM Trace supporting state and local COVID-19 Contact Tracing programs. Carolyn is currently part of the first cohort accepted into the American Nurses Association/California's Advocacy Institute fellowship program.

OUR DREAMS ARE OURS TO MAKE

INGRID DUQUE

"If your dreams do not scare you, they are not big enough."

"Good afternoon ladies and gentlemen, this is your captain speaking. On behalf of American Airlines, I would like to welcome you to Atlanta, Georgia. Please enjoy your visit and make some memories...." I can clearly remember the captain's words as if it were yesterday, but the reality is that it has been over twenty years since my family made the decision to leave our beloved country, Colombia, our family, our friends and embark on a new adventure.

We came to the United States, the land of opportunities, to chase the coveted "American Dream." As a ten-year-old, the experience of being in a new country, embracing a new culture, and learning a new language was intimidating, and, at times, scary. I remember spending hours trying to translate English reading assignments, word for word, just so that I could understand enough of the content in order to complete the homework assignments. It was challenging going to school every day, looking different from the 99% Anglo student body, and struggling to have a simple conversation with schoolmates and teachers.

High school came with a different set of challenges, and I found myself in the minority once again as one of three Latinos attending the school. I was also introduced to a group of acronyms that could have a significant impact on my dreams of becoming an engineer: AP, GPA, ACT, and SAT. When discussing these with my assigned counselor, she told me to not worry about them, and to reassess my engineering goal since it was "too big of a dream." I was confused. How could someone that did not know me make such an assessment? I made the decision that day to not let anyone set limits on my potential or dictate what I was capable of.

Fast forward three years when I graduated high school one month after my sixteenth birthday with a full-ride scholarship to my dream school, one of the top engineering schools in the country. I pursued both my undergraduate and graduate engineering degrees, and subsequently obtained my professional engineering license.

Throughout my professional career, I have had the opportunity to hold leading roles in multiple Fortune 500 companies, traveled the world, and collaborated with amazing individuals on one-of-a-kind projects. The little girl that was once afraid and intimidated by the sight of new challenges now embraces them. For all the girls and boys out there, do not let anyone tell you what you are capable of achieving, or that your dreams are too big; on the contrary, if your dreams do not scare you, they are not big enough. I am proof that as an immigrant, you can dare to dream of creating an extraordinary life and achieve it. *Sí se puede!*

BIOGRAPHY

Ingrid Duque, PE, was born in Cali, Colombia, and moved with her family to the United States when she was ten. She is a licensed professional engineer with an undergraduate degree in structural engineering and a graduate degree in engineering mechanics.

She has over eleven years of professional experience in leadership roles with Fortune 500 companies (Southern Company, Westinghouse Electric Company, Jacobs, and others), and serves as a top advisor for minority-led real estate development startups.

She currently works at Southern Nuclear Company, a group of nuclear energy facility operators and advanced nuclear technologies researchers, and leads the transition of Plant Vogtle Units 3 and 4 to Operations, the first new nuclear units built in the United States in more than three decades.

LETTING GO OF SELF-LIMITING VIEWS

SHAWN EDWARDS

"Personal growth is often accompanied with personal discomfort."

In 2019, I delivered the Columbia Engineering Class Day keynote. Reflecting on my education and career, I told my story as one of learning to let go of self-limiting views. I thank my mother for teaching me this.

She came to the United States from Quito, Ecuador, at sixteen. Like so many immigrants before her, she was forced to adapt and persist in new and sometimes uncomfortable situations. She attended high school in Brooklyn without speaking English, but managed to get straight As. After moving to Massachusetts with her mother and sisters, she met my father, a machinist. His blended French Canadian and Irish American family was rooted in Western Massachusetts. I grew up in two different cultures, having amazing grandmothers, one we called Mémé and the other, Abuelita.

My mother pursued her college degree while my three siblings and I were young. I fondly remember sitting in the back of a college lecture room drawing while she attended class. My mother cared for us, pursued a career, and went to school at night, eventually earning her master's in social work. During my freshman year of high school, my mother became the main income earner when my father was laid off, after the factory at which he worked for many years shut down.

She had an incredible work ethic and taught us the value of perseverance by example. Her fierce commitment to family and determination were always there for us to witness. She imbued in us this grounded sense of toughness, that we are capable of achieving our goals and to never feel sorry for ourselves.

All my siblings attended college before me, but only I pursued engineering. I knew little about this profession, and quickly realized how underprepared I was compared to other Columbia University students. College required serious determination for me to not back down.

My career followed suit. With my electrical engineering degree, I started in chip design at IBM, and returned to Columbia for my master's degree. I then worked at Mentor Graphics and Bear Stearns as a software engineer. I worked on increasingly complex programs, from small components to architecting large-scale, high-performance market data systems.

Every step along the way, I had to remind myself, "Wait a minute, I can do this." I translated my mother's numerous examples into a concrete personal directive of identifying and removing self-imposed limitations. Realizing that personal growth is often accompanied with personal discomfort, I put myself out there.

At Bear, I managed people, led projects, and built trading

systems. After meeting the head of front office technology, I knew I was just as capable. My ability to assume roles I initially didn't think were possible for someone like me still serves me to this day. I learned to lead teams and became a managing director.

Moving to Bloomberg, I gave all that up to become an individual contributor again—an uncomfortable and interesting challenge. Since then, I've worked my way to the top of our technical organization.

I've passed these lessons to my son and daughter—both of whom are also engineers. I tell them that, yes, they do belong, and that they should be mindful of unconsciously setting their own limits. As long as you work hard enough, there's no reason to stop yourself, establish barriers, or think that this is your place in life.

BIOGRAPHY

As Bloomberg's Chief Technology Officer, Shawn Edwards oversees its global technology strategy. His team partners with Bloomberg Engineering to develop the company's market data, analytics, news, and community products; research existing and emerging technologies; and architect strategic technical solutions—including enhancing its core business, the Bloomberg Terminal. Shawn advances Bloomberg's engagement with academia, including research fellowships, grants, and sponsorships, and leads engagement with open-source and developer communities.

Institutional Investor has repeatedly named him a top technology leader in finance. Shawn is Vice Chairman of Latino U College Access (LUCA), a nonprofit that helps Latino youth enroll and succeed in college.

TAKING CONTROL OF MY PERSONAL NARRATIVE

LUZELENA ESCAMILLA

"After that, I began to give myself a different identity and self-worth; I began to take control of my personal narrative."

One of the most prevalent memories from my childhood is waking up from my bed at midnight and continuing my rest before school in the backseat of my mom's car. When my family first moved to America, my mom worked delivering newspapers for the Chicago Tribune. We moved to this country without knowing anyone in it. That was one of the many hardships that my immigrant parents had to face upon arriving in the United States. They sacrificed their well-recognized careers in Mexico to ensure my brother and I receive the best education and opportunities.

Leaving our family and my parents' careers behind, we came to America to start all over and obtain the "American Dream." Seeing that my parents have sacrificed so much only made me work that much harder to succeed.

During my freshman year of community college, I was elected

student trustee of the second-largest institution in Illinois. With the humbling and honorary position that I upheld, I had many great opportunities. I had a surreal feeling one day when I stood in the headquarters of the *Chicago Tribune*, where I was invited to introduce our new college president. The power of education: from sleeping in my mom's car while she delivered *Chicago Tribune* newspapers to actually sitting in a landmark building in Chicago. After that, I began to give myself a different identity and self-worth, and I began to take control of my personal narrative.

My unending hunger for education and helping others find their passion through learning branched out a mission. A mission to see every single human being receive an equitable education. After pushing myself academically at community college, I continued my higher education at George Washington University in Washington, DC. and started working at organizations that are working towards education equity.

My first job was at Malala Foundation, co-founded by the youngest Nobel Prize laureate and Pakistani activist for female education, Malala Yousafzai. After that, I went on to work at an organization led by the tenth US Secretary of Education in President Barack Obama's cabinet, Dr. John B. King Jr. These experiences and opportunities made me realize that this was all possible because I never let societal stigmas faze me.

I was taking control of the narrative that I wanted to create for myself. It did not matter to me that I was born in Mexico, that English was my second language, and that I did not have the family connections to land my dream job—that encouraged me to work ten times harder. I knew I believed in my passion, that education is a universal human right, and no human should be deprived of it.

I witnessed firsthand how education helped me obtain an identity and discover my strengths. I continue to take control of my personal narrative today by advocating for equitable education and using innovation to address this challenge. I tell my story to inspire others to create their own personal narrative, to pursue their passions and leave an impact in our world today.

BIOGRAPHY

Luzelena Escamilla is a social impact activist, storyteller, and innovator. Her passion and career have been centered around advocating for a gender-equal world through building social impact initiatives and partnerships across various influential nonprofits, innovative companies, and international policies.

As a first-generation Latina woman, Luzelena has made it her mission to advocate for underserved communities and use innovation to address the world's greatest challenges.

LIVING TO THE MAX

MINDY ESCOBEDO

"Live life to the max."

Imagine sitting in an emergency room and hearing that you might be taking your last breaths. Every second, 1.8 people die in this world. Think of how easily that could be you. In October of 2019, I was given the news that I had an inch and a half of bleeding in my brain. The doctors told me that this could possibly kill me or soon put me in a vegetative state. I immediately thought my life was ending and could not stop crying. It seemed like there was a limit on everything I could do, and a time frame on when I could complete what I wanted in life.

I faced many challenges throughout this unknown time. Everything the doctors told me sounded foreign. My prescription was: bedrest and keep yourself from getting stressed. If you knew me, you'd understand that this is impossible. In the small time of rest that I took, following the doctor's orders, I gave up many events which included my initiation into my sorority.

Although I was keeping myself from staying extremely busy, I realized that work could still be done with or without being in the office. I learned to overcome my obstacles with the help of my family and friends. I was in a dark place of feeling useless, but they constantly made sure I felt that I was accomplishing what I needed to feel good about my physical and mental state at the time. After a few weeks of bedrest and throwing myself a pity party, I contemplated the value of life. I realized that no one knows when it is their time to leave this earth. So, I made a declaration to myself and my family: to always live life to the max.

I thank God for giving me this brain bleed. Without it I would not be who I am today. Because of this, I have learned to value time more and have taken on many more projects and leadership positions on my college campus and within my community.

I encourage all people to never give up when things go wrong. You will always come to a place where you will stop at obstacles in life, but it is how you face those obstacles that will determine how far you go. After gaining the courage to face life head-on, I have been proudly elected as president of my campus's LULAC (League of United Latin American Citizens), my sorority's vice president, named as an ambassador for my campus, have been chosen as an intern for a Texas State Representative, and received academic scholarships, all while working a full-time job that, at times, required me to work internationally and manage company projects valued at over a billion dollars. You will never know when it is your time to leave, so today, you should make decisions that will further your walk to success—and never look back.

BIOGRAPHY

Mindy Escobedo is a second-year student at Lamar University, vice president of her sorority, and the president of the collegiate LULAC of that campus.

At the age of nineteen, Mindy has already worked with international companies with projects valued at over one billion dollars. She has managed to go to work full-time, go to school full-time, and still serve actively on local nonprofits and campaigns. Mindy is also an intern for a Texas State representative and holds other leadership positions.

JOANNA FELICIANO

"No matter how hard it gets, you were made for more and have a purpose assigned to you for a time like this. I encourage you to change your narrative."

On a Monday morning in May 2017, I remember driving to Philadelphia to start my new job in a city I didn't know. During the drive, I reflected on the last nineteen months: of being unemployed for a long time from a corporate job and working two part-time jobs with one at a large retailer. This was one of the most challenging times of my life, during which I questioned my abilities, education, and life's purpose. Many questions were running through my mind, and as I sat at the new employee orientation, a voice kept saying I was made for more and needed to connect with my purpose. Little did I know that this moment would create a spark and a mission to connect with the purpose-driven Joanna inside me.

The nineteen months challenged my self-esteem, which I just wanted to quit after sending over three-hundred applications,

of wisdom, a cheerleader, a splash of cold water or a fire under our tail to get us going. Oftentimes, we don't know what we don't know—and that's where mentors matter. My journey hasn't been easy, but it became easier when others invested in me along the way. That's why I'm passionate about opening the doors for others.

BIOGRAPHY

Misty Fernandez is currently an area manager for Georgia Power. In this role, Misty works with local, regional, and state leaders to advance operational, economic, community development and charitable giving strategies for the north Atlanta area.

In the community, Misty serves on multiple nonprofit boards and serves as chair of the board of directors for the Latin American Association. She was recognized by the Hispanic Association of Corporate Responsibility as one of forty high-achieving Hispanics in the US and was recently named as one of the fifty Most Influential Latino Leaders in Georgia.

Georgia Power is the largest subsidiary of Southern Company, one of the nation's largest generators of electricity. The company is an investor-owned utility, serving 2.6 million customers in 155 of 159 counties in Georgia.

DANIEL FLORES

"You can do everything you put your mind to."

My name is Daniel Flores, and I was born in Mexico City twenty-seven years ago. My family moved to the United States when I was ten years old. I was raised by an amazing single mother, who I dedicate this story to. Being an immigrant, being raised by a single parent, and living below the poverty line was tough. At the same time, it helped me become more focused and push harder at a very young age.

Seeing the family struggle helped me develop a chip on my shoulder and the desire to make it in America. One thing I want to emphasize is that anything is possible through hard work, positivity, and perseverance. I was the kid selling my homework and knocking on doors to make some extra cash. I was also the quiet kid that didn't want problems, so I could avoid being a target for being a Mexican immigrant. I remember seeing other kids being bullied for it and talked down to.

As I got older, I realized that there is power in being you and being proud of where you come from. One of my goals became to work on myself in order to change how Mexican immigrants are viewed. We have courage and can do great things.

Education is a way to level the playing field. For that reason, I attended the University of Texas at Dallas. I could not afford it and did not qualify for financial assistance, but I found a way. I started a landscaping business. I used to mow eighteen lawns in one day. At the same time, I was a server, a sales rep, and had many internships. After grinding and pushing hard, I graduated debt free in 2015, with a finance degree. This unlocked many opportunities to come.

I began my corporate career in 2016 as a sales rep in the technology industry. That kid that used to sell homework in middle school somehow made it to the B2B tech sales world. I also co-founded a frozen food business which currently has shelf space at Foxtrot Market.

Currently, I'm in the process of launching a real estate venture with my best friend. It's exciting to know that Mexican immigrants can close big deals in corporate America, start small businesses, get into the real estate game, run marathons, and do whatever we put our minds to. My mother Iris always said to me, "You can do everything you put your mind to." And for that reason, I owe everything to her. For the ones reading, keep pushing.

BIOGRAPHY

Daniel Flores is a Mexican immigrant. He moved to the US

when he was ten years old. Raised by an amazing single mother, he is currently a field sales account executive at Hewlett-Packard Enterprise, where he helps large enterprises increase revenue, decrease costs, and mitigate risk with the help of technology.

Daniel is the co-owner of Momo Shack Dumplings, a booming food business in Dallas, Texas. He has entered the real estate game as ESL Properties and his goal is to build financial freedom, generational wealth, and empower the immigrant/minorities to do the same. He is a hybrid athlete and full-time hustler.

ROMELIA FLORES

"Performing as much as I can to the best of my abilities and having enjoyment are the key to success."

How does a young, Hispanic girl living in the sleepy, little Mexican border town of Eagle Pass, Texas go from working as an administrative assistant at a local hospital to becoming a distinguished engineer at IBM, having produced seventy-six patents and tremendously impacting the youth of today and tomorrow? It's an amazing story. This is the story of Romelia Flores' career.

I am the daughter of a milkman and a secretary, the two people I credit for my success. While my mother advised me to perform as much as I could to the best of my abilities, my father, on the other hand, advised me to do things that bring me enjoyment. I attended the University of Texas at Austin and obtained a degree in Computer Science. As an intern at IBM, writing code was challenging but fun. Using my mom's advice, my code was as close to perfection as possible, but I was also having fun, as my father would appreciate.

During my first fifteen years at IBM, I established a strong technical foundation, learning methodologies for designing, developing, and innovating highly functional and successful products. I developed products using assembler, COBOL, C, C++, and SmallTalk. As I reflect on the variety of products I created (3270 Data Streams, High Level Language Application Programming Interface [HLLAPI], and DB2/2), I smile at the fact that some clients are operating these technologies in production environments to this day. This strong technical foundation has benefited me in subsequent roles at IBM as a Technical Support Specialist, IT Consultant and Open Systems Solution Architect, and now as a Distinguished Engineer.

I enjoy being a continuous learner and inventor at IBM. I believe that technology evolves at such a rapid pace that an individual always needs to evolve their skills and be open to creative ways of staying at the "cutting edge." It is this challenge that I thrive on that has resulted in the seventy-six patents credited to my name.

Today, I embrace design thinking techniques to lead co-creation activities with my clients and colleagues. I see the impact that collaboration with diverse and empowered teams has on creating solutions and am a firm believer that this contemporary approach fuels innovation.

My largest impact on IBM technologists and external communities is the "giveback" I deliver. I have trained thousands of IBMers, university, high school, and middle school students, entrepreneurs, and innovators world-wide. At IBM, I lead Diversity & Inclusion for IBM's Academy (top technical leaders) and collaborate with top IBM Hispanic executives to nurture existing and future Hispanic talent.

I am delighted to be a role model in my community, and proudly serve on the Fort Worth Museum of Science and History Board, the Baylor Engineering and Computer Science Board of Advocates, the Dallas Alliance of Technical Women, and the International Women's Forum. It is evident that I have followed my mother and father's advice to do as much as I can, to the best of my ability, and to have fun doing it all!"

BIOGRAPHY

Romelia Flores is a distinguished engineer and master inventor. Her industry experiences combined with her unique software development and design expertise make her Global Markets' most highly sought-after innovator.

She has collaborated with leading clients in the design of Storm Water Management, Cloud Platform Delivery, Hepatitis C Eradication, and Airport Parking. She holds seventy-six US patents and has fifteen patents pending.

In 2018, Romelia was the first female ever named to the Dallas Tech Titan Hall of Fame and was the 2016 Lifetime Achievement Award winner from Great Minds in STEM.

ANDREA FREIRE KNUTH

*"Resilience, perseverance, and my entrepreneurial spirit gave
me the courage to follow my dreams; and embracing my family's
multicultural traditions always offered me new perspectives to
opportunities in the face of challenges."*

I was eighteen years old when I arrived in The United States of America. I thought I spoke English because I always got the highest grades in my English language classes while in high school, but then I realized I did not.

My mother moved to Ecuador when I was seven years old. I admired her for having the strength to make tough decisions, that, to me, always projected resilience and perseverance. Life was not easy for her migrating from Colombia to Ecuador to the United States. She never gave up, although she has always been very reserved. In my eyes, she has been the most courageous woman I have ever met. And she made sure I enrolled in college when I arrived.

Once in college, I decided to take ESL classes along with computer science classes. Back in high school, IT (Information Technology) was my elective profession, and I learned Cobol and Basic programing, and Windows 3.1. I was able to learn English as I studied programing languages and advanced math. Then I transferred to Fairleigh Dickinson University, where I got my bachelor's degree in computer science. I was one of two women, and the only Latina in the class of 2000 graduating with that degree.

But little did I know how challenging it was going to be to get a job in technology, and from perseverance I got my first job as a Java and web developer for the State of New Jersey. But there was still something more in me, in my heart, a desire to be an entrepreneur. Since I was a little girl, I had envisioned myself as a businesswoman, but at that time, business and IT where two different worlds.

My father is an entrepreneur. He opened his orthopedic and prosthetic business as a young man. He called me one day and asked me to help him run his business, but that meant quitting my secured technology job, leaving everything, and moving back to Ecuador. I remember thinking, "I have always dreamed of being an entrepreneur, so this is my opportunity to learn about business, and, even better, from my father."

So, I quit and moved back in 2007, went for a master's degree in business administration through online education—when that form of learning was still in its early stages. But I thought it was the future, and I wondered how it was structured.

As my journey became a mix of rough and clouded roads, and

I experienced situations that I never thought I would; I continued to grow my knowledge base, adding a certificate in business analytics from Harvard University, and making my entrepreneurial dream a reality where technology, analytics, and business are integrated. I never stopped being proud of being a Latina computer scientist and celebrate being a woman and wearing heels, even though I was constantly being told I was not the stereotype of a person (not to say a woman) in information technology. Resilience, perseverance, and my entrepreneurial spirit gave me the courage to follow my dreams, and embracing my multicultural traditions always offered new perspectives to opportunities.

BIOGRAPHY

Andrea Freire Knuth is the founder and CEO of Adalitika, LLC, specializing in providing data strategy solutions that are customer-centric, data-centric, and AI-centric, taking companies to the next level of their digital transformation journey.

Andrea has more than twenty years of professional experience as a software engineer, business analyst, general manager, director of development, and director of operations. She is also the co-founder and Deputy CEO of GIOSPORTEC S.A., a company dedicated to integrating technology, education, and sports for training and coaching athletes.

STEVE GALLEGOS

"I achieve my dreams by helping others achieve theirs."

I arrived home from school feeling sick to my stomach. Desperation, my faithful friend, accompanied me as I searched for a plastic bag. Epic Dry Cleaning was emblazoned on the bag; an appropriate tool to end my less than epic life. I sat on the edge of my bed and wrapped the bag around my head holding it tightly around my neck. Would it take fifteen seconds? Twenty seconds? I started becoming dizzy and once again heard that voice saying, "No, there's a better way." I removed the bag from my head and gasped for a huge breath of air.

Is there a better way? It was a question I asked repeatedly. I was seventeen years old, convinced by my parents that I was an absolute "good-for-nothing." The physical beatings and mental abuse were no match for the indifference with which I was treated over the years. I had no self-worth, no dreams, and no plans for the future.

I spied the bright blue book on the shelf loaned to me by

my high school girlfriend: "The Power of Positive Thinking," by Norman Vincent Peale. Although most of his ideas were beyond my understanding, I connected with seven words that inspired me to take my life in a new direction: I did not think it was possible to change my thoughts, but I knew I could change my world, having run away from home several times before. So, I joined the US Marine Corps.

In my training class, there were three Spanish-speaking recruits, who were struggling with the academics. Wanting them to succeed, I offered to help them master the material. So, when everyone had gone to sleep, the four of us would go into the showers and sit on the cold, damp, musty floor. Each night, I translated that day's training from English into Spanish and discussed it until they understood. No one asked me to help them. I was not a teacher. It was something I had to do.

Two weeks into our nightly tutoring, we were caught by surprise as our on-duty drill instructor descended upon us with the delicacy of a rogue bull protecting his territory. Storming into the showers, screaming at the top of his lungs, we tried to blend in with the tiles on the floor. I caught my breath, placed my heart inside my chest and jumped up to explain the situation. Glaring at us in disbelief, he said, "Carry on."

On the final exam, I scored the highest in the class, and my three friends ranked among the top ten. I was named the Honor Graduate, promoted to Private First Class, and awarded the coveted Dress Blue Uniform, for which the US Marines are known worldwide.

I was not the strongest, nor the fastest, nor the most intelligent. I simply chose to help another human. From this experience my life's motto was born: "I achieve my dreams, by helping others achieve theirs."

BIOGRAPHY

Regarded as America's Ambassador on Success, Steve Gallegos guides others on how to experience greater self-mastery, communications-mastery, and relationship-mastery. These are the three pillars to living remarkably, a proven philosophy that will guide you to experience a life beyond your limitations.

Through lessons earned as a US Marine Sergeant, law enforcement officer, singer-songwriter and recording artist, board-certified civil trial lawyer, and published commercial photographer, Steve is on a mission to elevate others, so that we may all contribute to society at a higher level.

Through his thought-provoking and inspirational stories, delivered in English or Spanish, Steve inspires his audiences to shed their limiting beliefs and take inspired action to achieve what otherwise seems impossible.

Steve is an award-winning author, international speaker, and joint venture specialist and serves as president of The Stevie G. Success Group, offering experiential public speaking training for executives, entrepreneurs, and professional service providers.

A CALLING FROM WITHIN

RUBY GARCIA

"Your career gives you something to live on, but your calling gives you to something to live for."

I had a very personal connection to foster care. First, my niece had entered the foster care system as an infant and was placed in the guardianship of her maternal grandmother, and second, I had previously spent seven years advocating for abused and neglected children in the local child welfare system. This work was more than just a job to me; it was a calling.

The day I received my official fellowship award, I was elated. After a grueling seven-month selection process, I was offered a role with a Washington, DC-based agency. I was one of ten selected out of three hundred for an opportunity to bring my leadership and business skills into the social sector, with the intention of building a movement to positively transform the child welfare system. I could not have been more optimistic about my future, even if it meant leaving the Chicago suburbs after forty years.

Imagine my disappointment when, six months into my new role, I realized it was not the right fit for me. I wondered why I had invested so much of my time and energy into something that wouldn't work out.

Callings rarely make sense. It took courage to pursue something I didn't fully understand. Callings aren't found through logic, analysis, or intellect. Callings speak through the heart. They are temporary and naturally evolve over time to reflect how we are also transforming. I had to trust this was the case with my fellowship experience. The resignation of my role became the redirection of my call.

As a single mother, it would have made sense to return to Chicago where I had family, but for years I had felt drawn to North Carolina. There was nothing waiting for me in North Carolina, except a deep inner knowing that it was the next place to call home.

Despite loving precautions from family, I chose to create a life in North Carolina with my two sons. My decision didn't make sense to others, but only I can hear what my heart is speaking. It was up to me to discern the voice from within and to choose whether I pursued my next divine assignment or not.

My callings have become an adventure I look forward to and an expression of my life's purpose: to inspire and support others in their journeys. Each time, my calling has stretched me and taken me out of my comfort zone, both literally and figuratively. Each calling has prepared me for the next assignment.

The systemic work I learned through my fellowship prepared me for the work I did alleviating food insecurity as the community engagement director of a local nonprofit. That work would lead me to promoting equity and justice through the school district and the township's advisory boards. My career always gave me something to live on, but my callings have given me something to live for: the opportunity to build a legacy, where I can positively influence those around me wherever I go.

BIOGRAPHY

Ruby Garcia has always had a desire to make a positive contribution to the world, so it is no surprise that she found her life's work in helping others fulfill their callings as a leadership and life coach. Ruby believes that to transform our communities, we must first transform ourselves. She is the founder of Ruby Garcia Coaching, and the creator of Woman Warrior Within, a training program for women who desire to tap into their power and use their influence to make positive impact.

She is a devoted mother, proud Latina, spiritual alchemist, and social justice warrior.

OSCAR GARCIA

"One person with courage is a majority."

My parents were Mexican immigrants. I was born in California. Like many kids, I grew up wanting a normal life. I wanted to fit in. I wanted to do things and go places like my friends. But my life was different. *Mi cultura* was different. *Mi familia* was different. I spoke a different language. Society told me that I was different. I was told that I was a minority. I started kindergarten speaking only Spanish. I was in ESL classes until the third grade. I remember being embarrassed every time my ESL teacher pulled me out of class.

Each of us has our own story; our own struggles; our own victories; our own purpose. My purpose is to serve, encourage, and help others. These ideals have been passed on from generation to generation, redefined by my experiences and cemented in my heart from the joy of triumphing over adversity.

Have you ever worked hard for something and then were told

that you received the promotion because you're a minority? I had good grades, and my high school counselor asked what I wanted to do after graduating. I'm a first-generation professional. My dad had a first-grade education. My mother finished middle school. I didn't know where I wanted to go to college. Against my counselor's recommendation, I applied to UC Berkeley and other UC schools. Guess what? The first school that accepted me was UC Berkeley. Oh, what a feeling!

I was actually accepted to all the universities I applied to. As admission letters started arriving, and word spread where everyone was going to college, I heard from some classmates that the only reason I was accepted to UC Berkeley was because of affirmative action; because I was a minority.

As I reflect on my upbringing, I realize that I am a minority. We tend to associate the word minority with being part of an ethnic group. I am proud of my Mexican heritage. I am proud to stand on the shoulders of my BIPOC brothers and sisters, anyone who has gone before me and helped smash the walls of prejudice and discrimination. But I realize that I am a minority because few people, regardless of their ethnicity, race, gender, or socioeconomic level, believe they can make a difference.

The majority believes they are too busy to make a difference. They believe they need a special talent or education. They believe they need to know the right people. One person with courage is a majority. God does not make junk. You and I were created for greatness. I realize that whatever my challenge is, there is always someone who has overcome the same challenge—or greater. It is our attitude that helps us to persevere, despite the odds. It is our willingness to get up one more time than we've been knocked down. It is our compassion for others—to see a need and with passion dedicate all our efforts to filling that need—that sets you and me apart from the majority.

BIOGRAPHY

Oscar Garcia is the Founder and Chief Empowerment Officer of Aspira Consulting, a Silicon Valley training and consulting firm. He is an introvert turned international speaker.

His career journey includes business development roles at five startups, co-founding a nonprofit, Chamber President and CEO, and Community Partnerships Manager at LinkedIn.

He's trained over 20,000 professionals across five continents. His training style is of a "practrainer" —he actively practices what he trains others to do. He is also the host of the dynamic and engaging podcast "Career Talk With OG." As Chief Empowerment Officer, Oscar empowers you, so opportunities come to you.

MYRNA GARCIA

"Being in your purpose is a true blessing."

Upon reflecting on my twenty-five years in corporate America, I asked myself, "What do I want to do for the last ten years of my career?" As a Latina, I had enjoyed a fruitful career that provided economic stability and cemented my personal brand; however, I was not engaged or integrated with my Latino/Hispanic community. I wanted to do more for my community in the last ten years of my career. That epiphany changed my career trajectory, shaped my legacy, and has helped me realize that being in your purpose is a blessing!

When the opportunity emerged for me to work in the nonprofit space at the Georgia Latin American Association (LAA), my initial thought was, "You cannot afford my payroll demands." Their very wise and great leader suggested that the position to lead fund development, communications, and volunteer initiatives aligned perfectly with my many years in strategic sales, but also with my personal goals and mission. She assured me the compensation would be attractive, and that when you do what you love, the rewards will follow.

I made the life-changing decision to transition into the nonprofit sector at LAA and loved every moment of it. After three and a half years, I transitioned to INROADS, an international nonprofit organization that creates pathways to careers for ethnically diverse high school and college students across the country.

Now, eight years later, I am privileged to make an impact in the lives of those we serve. As the AVP strategic account management and business development and head of national Hispanic initiatives at INROADS, I lead a wonderful team of individuals that achieve unrestricted revenue and have impacted over 150 thousand interns across the country. Our leadership development programs and services across the continuum make an impact in driving results while supporting DEI and talent pipelines across more than 200 partners across the nation.

As head of national Hispanic initiatives, I have the privilege to impact my community while also supporting African American, Native American, and Pacific Asian demographics. The mission of INROADS is to deliver innovative leadership development programs and creative solutions that identify, accelerate, and elevate underrepresented talent throughout their careers.

COVID-19 and the racial awakening of the country has impacted each of our individual communities. It has made all of us reflect on our personal contributions to society and our call to make the world a better place.

I feel so blessed to have the opportunity to impact the lives of others. I encourage you to appreciate the many pathways your career may take. Embrace these changes as you find your purpose. Focus on how you can make a difference and positive impact on anything you touch. Being a signatory to the initiatives of "WE ARE ALL HUMAN" is another way to make an impact for the betterment of ALL. Being in your purpose is a true blessing.

BIOGRAPHY

Myrna Garcia is the assistant vice president of strategic account management and business development at INROADS, Inc., a nonprofit organization. Her team accounts for over 60% of the total revenue of the enterprise.

Additionally, Myrna leads national Hispanic strategies for INROADS. Her professional background spans over thirty-five years in strategic sales, executive placement, contingent workforce management solutions, diversity, and inclusion, as well as fund development and marketing communications.

Myrna has many awards and affiliations, most recently a signatory to the Hispanic Promise, "WE ARE ALL HUMAN," and serves on several advisory boards.

LILIANA GUTIERREZ

"Making assumptions about people, their looks, and their languages can be a fast recipe for mistakes."

I finished high school in Colombia, learning French and English, with many subjects delivered in French. I wanted to be a translator and needed to improve my conversational English, which led me to be interested in an exchange program. It was a big step to entrust a rather young and over-protected daughter to live in another country, and I had a wonderful experience, including living with my family for a year after.

My idea of career and college location evolved because of this. Being away increased the value of being close to family vs. going to college in Europe. Two uncles attended the University of Texas in Austin, and I decided to go there with one of my brothers, who was a year younger. We would both start in the school of engineering at the same time, given my year in the United States with my exchange family.

The freshman orientation was held in a large auditorium, with hundreds of international students. My brother and I sat together, a bit nervous to be at UT in the huge room amid many people from all over the world. The day started with speakers from various departments, titles, and areas of the school, and it became a long and boring session.

This is where I learned a lifelong lesson! We were the only ones who looked like we were from South America, with some empty seats next to us, so we thought we had a comfortable zone of privacy. While speakers were droning on, we started to write each other notes and comment in low voices. Soon, our comments grew to be silly.

To our surprise, a kid just a few seats away kept snickering and at one point, started laughing out loud after one of our snarky comments. He looked like someone from Asia, so we assumed he was from Asia and would not understand Spanish. Bad assumption! He was from Panama, and very much a fellow Latino with perfect Spanish, mannerisms, and culture. We only figured it out when he made a comment back and we met him during a break. It is now a funny, if embarrassing, moment, and a memory that has stayed with me and influenced me all these years.

Since then, I've also become very aware that you just cannot make assumptions when it comes to language in either direction. My children have Spanish first names, but they have different levels of Spanish fluency. People do make assumptions based on their names. It's important to be aware in our daily lives that names, looks, and location do not necessarily correlate to language or other skills. I have been the recipient of people assuming I don't understand French or even English in my travels, so it goes both ways.

I continue to be grateful I learned a valuable lesson that has helped me in life, while traveling and working with people in a global company. Making assumptions about people, their looks, and their languages can be a fast recipe for mistakes!

BIOGRAPHY

Liliana Gutierrez is originally from Cali, Colombia, and has lived in various states in the US. She has an engineering in business undergraduate degree and an MBA, with ongoing education in technology, industries, and other topics.

Liliana has worked in different roles, from technical to sales and now global sales enablement. She is fluent in Spanish and English and comfortable with French. She is married, has two adult children, and currently enjoys her work while living by a lake. Liliana volunteers in the community and likes to hike, travel, quilt, and read.

KARLA HERNANDEZ DECUIR

"If you simply persist, you can achieve higher."

My story begins at the age of twelve, when I clearly recall speaking to my father, who was an attorney in Guatemala. I walked into his office, and he said to me, *"Mija,* knowledge is power, never forget that!" A few months later, my father would be murdered by what we believe was a government cover-up for a high-ranking court case he was overseeing.

I can now speak about it because so many years have passed, but I never spoke about it before. A few days after my father's funeral, we arrived in Houston, Texas, on a trip I thought was a simple visit. My mother, my sister, and I later moved to Louisiana, where my mother had found some long-lost relatives. My *tía* Ana was there to welcome us, and my mother soon found a school for us to attend. I then realized that this was not a short trip, but a total life change.

I found it hard to get used to not being with friends and family, and it seemed impossible to learn a new language in a place where I simply didn't feel welcome.

As I think back, I recall becoming my senior class's homecoming queen and graduating, but I don't recall applying to numerous universities or being too concerned about college. I simply knew that I needed to go to college because my dad would expect me to do so. It was very difficult to have to figure things out on my own because my mother didn't speak English and I truly didn't have anyone who could help besides my sister, who knew almost as much as I did about college in the United States. However, I persisted.

During my last semester at the University of New Orleans, Hurricane Katrina flooded the City of New Orleans, and we were forced to relocate once again. I can still feel the cold floors of the church's gymnasium where we had to shelter for a few days during that time. My mother, my sister, and I persisted and remained together. We decided to relocate to Houston, Texas, to start over again.

In Houston, I changed my perspective, and I became determined to do more, to become better, and to achieve higher. I went through a few obstacles to find a way to complete my last semester, and I completed my bachelor's degree in 2006. I became pregnant that semester, but I persisted and finished. I soon began working at the University of Phoenix, where I found a passion for higher education. I decided to enroll in a master's program, and I actually completed two master's degrees. I was ready for more.

In 2016, I moved to the University of Houston-Victoria to oversee a new instructional site in Katy, Texas as the executive director. I realized that in many meetings, I was the only Hispanic, the youngest, and one of the few females. During my first year, a dear mentor told me that if he could go back in time and do anything differently, it would be to earn a doctorate degree, and so I decided to find a program and apply. It was difficult to have two children under ten, to work full-time, and to enroll in a doctorate program, but I persisted. I knew that I would have to sacrifice time with my kids and with my family, so I decided to enroll full-time to finish faster.

In 2020, against the COVID-19 odds, I successfully defended my doctoral thesis, and I completed a Doctor of Education in Professional Leadership with an emphasis in Special Populations. I am now the highest-ranking Latina at my institution, and my supervisor is the highest-ranking Latino.

My position allows me to create strategies to make higher education more accessible to more students from all backgrounds. I am empowered to motivate and encourage students, especially Latino students, to attend college and to learn that if you simply persist, you can achieve higher.

BIOGRAPHY

As an immigrant from Guatemala City, Karla Hernandez DeCuir arrived in the US at the age of twelve to become the highest-ranking Latina at a state university. She grew up in the city of New Orleans and in 2006, after Hurricane Katrina, moved to Houston, Texas, where she now lives with her husband, two kids, and mother.

She graduated with a Bachelor's in Marketing from the University of New Orleans, she earned an MBA and a Master of Management in Human Resource Management from the University of Phoenix, and she recently completed a Doctor of Education in Professional Leadership from the University of Houston.

GABY HERNÁNDEZ FRANCH

"Be open to the possibilities."

I was in disbelief that I had made it this far, only to realize that it was not what I wanted at all. I was in my senior year of college, and I decided that after four years of studying biology and being in a pre-med track, I didn't want to pursue medicine anymore and I was done taking science courses. My world felt like it was crumbling down, and I had a knot of confusion in my heart about what I was supposed to do. It felt like a quarter-life crisis.

Being a first-generation Hispanic college student and the first person in my family to be graduating from college, I felt like a failure. How could I let go of a dream that I had for so long and had invested so much time and resources into? It was not only my dream, but also my parents' dream to see their daughter become a doctor. It was truly one of the scariest and most confusing times in my life.

It was so difficult that I ended up taking a semester off because

I had to address my anxiety and depression as a result of that decision. I was very confused and, overall, it was a grieving process. Ultimately, I could not envision myself going through four more years of medical school and pursuing a career that didn't have my full heart.

Fast forward three years later: I am now working in a completely different field, doing something that I never would have imagined I'd be doing. I work for a publishing and multimedia company, where I get to help others share their stories through books, events, and marketing. I love that I get to work with storytellers and be part of authors' magical journeys of creating a piece of work.

In retrospect, I am so glad that I followed my heart and was open to the idea that my dreams were changing—and leading elsewhere. I won't say it was easy and that I knew exactly what I was doing. I doubted myself, felt like my mind was jumbled, and I didn't believe in myself too much afterwards. But I didn't give up; I tried new industries like finance and education, where I learned valuable skills and knowledge and even discovered new parts of myself. I am a firm believer that every experience I go through brings new opportunities for growth and learning.

Now, I can confidently say I am happy that life led me where it needed me. It needed me to experience a "redirection," so that I could see that my journey is ever-changing, and I have gifts in this world to share in new ways than I thought possible. I am excited to keep exploring and cultivating my skills to better serve the world. I have added a new mantra to my life: "Be open to the possibilities," and so far, it's brought amazing blessings and opportunities to my life.

BIOGRAPHY

Gaby Hernández Franch is a first-generation college graduate from the University of Illinois at Chicago, and currently works at Fig Factor Media (FFM), an international multimedia and publishing house. Most recently, Gaby was named as a "30 Under 30" Honoree from the Publicity Club of Chicago and received the "Rising Star in Marketing" award for her professional accomplishments.

Gaby enjoys taking the stage as an MC for events and hosting the Author Central Podcast—FFM's very own podcast. She is very passionate about traveling, learning about cultures, and has a deep love for music and the arts. She happily lives with her wonderful husband Donald.

DR. ANNA FLORES LOCKE

"Living in shame and guilt with resentment is a dark place to be—I much prefer living in the light."

The infertility beast reared its nasty head and invaded my marriage from day one. After we professed our commitment to one another during a Roman Catholic ceremony, we were ready to have a child. So, right away we started. For three long years, we tried without success. Every month when I got my period, I'd sadly say, "No baby this time," to which my husband would reply, "We will try again, and it will happen in time."

Time ticked away and I became more and more obsessed and consumed with trying to get pregnant. We tried timed intercourse (which is having sex during my most fertile time of the month), we tried natural fertility enhancers (like herbs and medications), we tried "just relaxing." Nothing worked!

From this place of despair and desperation, our marriage

became tumultuous and fraught with blame and helplessness. We didn't know what else to do to achieve this life goal of having a baby. That is when we entered the world of reproductive medicine and invasive procedures to manipulate my body into a conception. After one emotionally and physically intense year of fertility treatments, including intra-uterine artificial insemination (IUI) and in-vitro fertilization (IVF), we conceived our first and only pregnancy. I gave birth after a high-risk pregnancy, leading to a hospitalization for eight weeks, to a boy and a girl. They were born prematurely and stayed in the neo-intensive care unit (NICU) for four weeks before coming home.

Achieving our dream of a family did not come easy for us. I struggled for many years to make sense of this atypical (but not abnormal) family-building journey. Why me? Why was it so hard? Being infertile was a shameful secret that I kept locked up.

I didn't want to face the medical diagnosis of infertility. I was in denial, and if I spoke about it, it would become real, and I would have to face it. I didn't want to appear weak or unworthy. Then one day, I made a decision: I could continue living with shame and regret, or I could live with pride and joy. I chose the latter.

I now realize that God led me to this unique doorway towards conception to show me my life's purpose. Being infertile is part of who I am, that I no longer hide. My passion to support others who have infertility warrant that I come out of the shadows. Living in shame and guilt with resentment is a dark place to be—I much prefer living in the light.

Sharing my story of infertility, telling others that my children were conceived through IVF, and being vocal on social media about it is liberating and empowering. At the age of forty, I have found my life's purpose through infertility, and I am fulfilled.

BIOGRAPHY

Dr. Anna Flores Locke is an assistant professor in a graduate mental health counseling program at Nyack College, owner of Charlandra Counseling Services, an author, and a social justice leader and advocate.

For many years after struggling with infertility herself before conceiving her twins through IVF, she has committed to supporting others along their family-building journey. She created the Fertility Clarity© approach to fertility counseling, to take the confusion and regret out of the journey, and to empower those living with infertility to make informed decisions that they can live with. She has found her life's purpose through infertility.

FROM THE FIELDS TO THE
BOARDROOM, ALWAYS GIVING BACK

JUAN LONGORIA

*"If you are going to do something, learn how to do it well. Then
make it easier for others to follow your path."*

In the late springs of the early 1980s, my family piled into an
old, white van. My grandfather drove while my grandmother said a
prayer and blessed us all before our two-day journey from San Benito,
Texas, to Kaleva, Michigan.

We arrived in a dust-filled camp of small houses with a shared
set of showers in the center. It was rare to have more than a day before
we started working in the fields. I was one of the youngest, so my
duties were less demanding, but I never felt like I had it easy. The
experiences we faced in the fields and the way people treated us in
the city followed me through my young adult life. When people
complained about simple tasks, I couldn't help but think that they'd
never had the chance to learn what real hard work was, like I did. I
didn't love school, but my mother reminding me that I could end up
in the fields for the rest of my life was more than enough motivation
to get a proper education.

After graduating high school, I did what most in their twenties do: have fun. I started bartending to make money; however, this led me astray from continuing my education or thinking about my future. At twenty-three, I realized I didn't want to bartend for the rest of my life, and I got a job at a call center. This was meant to be a short-term job, to help pay for tuition until I found my calling. The advice of my grandfather, however, always stayed with me. "If you are going to do something, learn how to do it well. Then make it easier for others to follow your path."

I found myself getting quickly promoted, then being recruited at different companies. In five years, I'd been able to go from answering tech support calls for dial-up internet, to running special projects for DISH Network. Five years after that, I was working for T-Mobile and on my way to leading partnerships across the globe for some of our largest call centers while earning my MBA. I'd turned a call center job into a career. It also gave me the flexibility and capital to start REVJLO, my own nonprofit in South Texas.

Through REVJLO, we've helped keep kids off the streets and given them a start to college when their parents couldn't afford it. While REVJLO continues working hard for communities, that passion for giving back has come full circle in my professional life as well.

Now, as a director at T-Mobile, I am also the co-chair for the LatinX ERG. I am honored to represent the thousands of ERG members, to be an advocate for change in representation and an example that, regardless of where you started, what you look like, or what you sound like, there is opportunity for everyone. My goal now is to continue to help my fellow Latinos and Latinas to achieve their version of success while proudly being themselves. I sincerely hope yours is too.

BIOGRAPHY

While starting off as a migrant worker in his childhood years, Juan Longoria is now the executive director and founder of REVJLO Charities in South Texas. Since 2012, their mission has been to remove obstacles to opportunity. REVJLO has provided close to $100 thousand in scholarships and has helped more than five hundred families in South Texas.

In addition to being a philanthropist, Longoria is the co-chair of the Latinx ERG and a director at T-Mobile. He has over twenty-two years of leadership experience in customer experience centers and BPO management. Juan has combined his experiences and is finding new ways to give back.

BE AN INTENTIONAL UNICORN

JENNIFER LOPEZ

"Now, instead of hiding my horn, I embrace that I am a unicorn—a very intentional one!"

I am grateful for my parents. They have always been supportive of both my passions: arts and academics. I was able to pursue and grow two careers—one as a professional dancer and fitness instructor and another as a chemical engineer.

I come from Puerto Rico, where there is a ton of emphasis on teamwork, hard work, familia, humor, charisma, and celebration. Imagine my surprise when I moved to the United States for graduate school. Upon seeing three ladies at school, no Latinx, I received the following "welcoming" comment after I introduced myself: "University of Puerto Rico, is that even a real university? How did you even get here?" followed by everyone laughing.

Moving out of my parents' house in a different country with a different language and different culture was one of the most difficult challenges that I had to navigate. But graduating with my master's degree gave me a great sense of confidence. That's when I learned to look back to grab that confidence, by reminding myself that if I was able to navigate through that, I can do anything!

That chapter was the beginning of a long career journey, trying to find myself again. In my professional career, I tried to mold, act, speak, and think like everyone else. I thought that was my only shot at achieving my goals. I constantly received comments like, "You need to dress like an engineer," "You are too bubbly," "I do not trust your leadership style," "You empower your employees too much," and "You need to be aware of first impressions, because you do not look smart," which did not help the situation.

Another aspect I struggled with was showing my true self. At work I was a leader; outside of work I was an NFL cheerleader and Zumba master trainer. That's when I felt like a unicorn that was sticking out, but not for the right reasons. At one point I thought I had to choose one to be successful. I thought revealing my other true side in each career was going to play against me. That was a limiting and disempowering belief, because what side do I choose? All sides made me, ME!

That's when a mentor told me simply: "Keep doing both! Do you realize that each career is making the other one stronger?" He was right! I needed to bring all of me every day! That was the secret sauce. That is the true meaning of diversity and inclusion. I realized that there was nothing wrong with me. My leadership style was influenced by my Latinx heritage; that was something to be proud of and a style that is very much needed in today's changing times.

From this learning point, my careers elevated—I found my

WHY—working with passion, so the next generations (including my two kids) can go to a workplace where they can shine without feeling like swimming against the current. Now, instead of hiding my horn, I embrace that I am a unicorn—a very intentional one!

BIOGRAPHY

Jennifer Lopez is from Puerto Rico and moved to the US to complete her MS in chemical engineering. Her engineering career includes roles in manufacturing, quality, and business, and she is currently senior director leading global recruiting for Eli Lilly. Jennie is a board member for the Organization of Latinx at Lilly, and a board of directors member for Genesis Research.

Her experiences in her dancing and fitness careers include: back up dancer for Ednita Nazario and Julio Iglesias, NFL cheerleader/captain, fitness instructor, and Zumba master trainer.

Jennie was awarded the 2020 Working Mother of the Year. She enjoys making intentional memories with her family.

LISEET LUNA-GUZMAN

"I was not wise enough when I was young to know that my humble beginnings would empower the passion within me to help others."

I am originally from El Paso, Texas. My family came from humble beginnings, originating from Mexico. Both of my parents worked to sustain a normal household. When I was in middle school, my mother and father lost their jobs and we lived for many years with financial hardships.

I remember thinking they were both working so hard and yet not really enjoying life. It inspired my drive and passion to do more from a young age. At times I felt embarrassed about our small apartment and that financially I could not always participate in school activities. I also felt embarrassed that my father struggled to speak English, and I always had to translate. Once my mother caught me complaining, and she said you can either feel sorry for yourself or leverage what blessings we did gift you. She said if I truly want to be someone who makes a difference, I need to leverage my strengths, such as speaking two languages, to help others. I was not wise enough at the time to understand, but eventually evolved into who I would become.

After attending New Mexico State University, I decided I needed to move somewhere where I could begin my life story and find my passion. I moved to Chicago and landed a job as a personal banker, where my love for small business banking began. I then went on to become a successful small business banker and that eventually evolved to becoming an award-winning leader of many successful teams—and, of course, the highlight of my life was getting married and having my own two children.

I truly believe everything does happen for a reason. I was not wise enough when I was young to know that my humble beginnings would empower the passion within me to help others. My mother was right: I was blessed that I could speak two languages, and this has allowed me to help many more people, which is a gift. I am true to myself, and I am a proud Latina. I am an encourager and developer of my team, other leaders, colleagues, and, of course, my family and friends. I want my team and the people in my life to be successful in all aspects of their lives and know that you can do anything you want if you're passionate and driven.

I also understand adversity and challenges that come from being an immigrant or any other non-traditional background, and now instead of running away from it, I embrace it and own it. This has made me a successful Latina woman leader. My hope is to continue to encourage our current and younger generation of Latinx, that *sí se puede* with hard work, and never be embarrassed about where you came from—instead, embrace it!

BIOGRAPHY

Liseet Luna-Guzman is a business banking specialist sales manager in the Chicago area for US Bank. She leads a team of small business banking specialists that assist small business owners. Her passion is developing and inspiring others to achieve their goals.

She is a member and leader of different groups within US Bank, a mentor for Girls with Impact along with a volunteer and advocate for local city programs that offer skill building for the future and current Latinx generation workforce. She feels a true leader always has a servant heart and is always looking for ways to do more!

THE SPIRIT OF THE LATIN AMERICAN

ALVARO LUQUE

"When we left Latin America for the US, we brought a spirit of determination and grit with us that has not dissolved in the American melting pot."

Latin America is a mosaic. I was born in Costa Rica, but I've also lived in Mexico and Venezuela, and worked closely with five countries in Central America. Every Latin American country represents different opportunities, cultures, and people—they're all very unique from one another. No two pieces of the mosaic are identical.

But having experienced so many of its parts firsthand, I've learned that they are all united under a common banner: perseverance. Every Latin American has endured crisis. Every single one of our countries has been challenged by a variety of complex problems. That's why Hispanics in the United States are fighters. When we left Latin America for the US, we brought a spirit of determination and grit with us that has not dissolved in the American melting pot.

When I was at the University of Costa Rica, I applied for a job at the biggest paper company in Central America, Scott Paper Company. I had no experience, but I also had no fear of rejection. I got the job because I was committed to excel, and that ignited my professional career. Since then, I've worked in a variety of leadership positions, even though I was younger than the others on my level.

Such professional success would not have been possible without my experience, my upbringing, and the hustling spirit that is instilled in every Latin American. Harnessing that spirit has been crucial in the different leadership positions I've held over the years for Hispanic brands like Gruma's Maseca and Mission Foods. My ambition paid off: In 2014, I was tapped to create a brand from the ground up to represent the Mexican avocado industry in the US and promote the fruits of 29,000 hardworking avocado farmers in Michoacán. It was the perfect opportunity to show the world what a driven spirit can accomplish.

Today, Avocados From Mexico (AFM) is the most popular brand of avocado in the US. Our small team has accomplished monumental things by channeling the same essence taught to me by my Latin American upbringing—at AFM, we call that spirit "Mexicanity." The spirit of Mexicanity is encoded in our brand's DNA. It uses the power of family, resilience, and good times to inspire and amplify the bonds, laughter, festivity, and success of everyone who works here. AFM has only existed for seven short years, but it stands as a powerful testament to the fruits of hard work.

My story is just one example of how a fighting spirit can

propel us to new heights, help us achieve great things, and break the traditional mold. That spirited trajectory is present in the stories of many Hispanic people, like the ones in this very book. The essence of the mosaic is within us—where will it take you?

BIOGRAPHY

Alvaro Luque is the CEO and president of Avocados From Mexico (AFM), the top avocado brand in the US. Under his leadership, AFM has led the growth of US avocado consumption to more than 2.5 billion pounds per year.

Alvaro's vision for making AFM the first fresh produce brand to advertise in the Super Bowl is one of many industry firsts that have positioned the brand as one of the most innovative produce companies in the world.

With over twenty-eight years of marketing experience, Alvaro has spent his professional career in leadership positions in the US and across Latin America.

I NEED TO KNOW OUR VOICES ARE HEARD

EDWINA MORALES

"Work towards striking the "NT" inside your head and heart."

Born and raised in New York, in a multigenerational Hispanic household, I am proud of my Puerto Rican roots and diverse upbringing. I found my purpose in advocating for those often overlooked, in this case, the powerful and influential multicultural consumer. Understanding the need for marketing practices to be inclusive and culturally relevant is imperative, not optional, not only drives my ethos when engaging with brands, but was the spark that shifted my career path.

This personal passion is what led me to join the multicultural practice at Horizon Media in 2018—after working on behalf of general market-focused brands for ten years.

My commitment to drive inclusive media practices in the industry has allowed me to lead purposeful projects, one example being the introduction of the Non-Discrimination of Media Vendors training based on the 2018 4As Fair Play Charter. This has been refreshed to incorporate the newly released five-point commitments in support of equitable consideration and investment with BIPOC media. As part of this initiative, I now sit on the 4As committee tasked with striking the "general market" and introducing a new, inclusive approach to planning and buying diverse audiences for the industry.

As a result, in 2020, one of my greatest accomplishments was in aiding the successful Potential Energy Coalition's "Vote Like a Madre" campaign by applying a cultural-first lens approach to activate Hispanic women to vote. Connecting the different layers of culture and developing 360 partnerships with trusted cultural authorities made #VLM feel a part of the target audience's broader Hispanic culture; creating a movement by infiltrating Hispanic culture, using tactics and channels that connect with Latinas in an authentic way.

Despite COVID-19 and the cluttered 2020 election media environment, this campaign ultimately influenced more than 550K Latinas to register and more than 800K Latinas to vote in a key presidential swing state, Arizona.

I also had the opportunity to take client segment planning to new levels in 2020, by partnering with Horizon's internal client teams to reinvent multicultural storytelling by re-evaluating audiences, media plans, buys, and creative through a sharper multicultural lens. This led to the creation of a four-part Multicultural Workshop series customizable for brands, which resulted in increased investments across minority-owned and targeted media and set the stage for additional diverse segment planning in 2021 across key brands within finance, health and wellness, insurance, and QSR. As a result of the Multicultural Workshop, brands specifically focused on Hispanic- and Black-owned and targeted networks, with a 200% year over year increased investment.

My commitment to drive inclusion extends beyond media and motivates me every day. By embedding myself within the Horizon DEI DNA as a member of the UNIDOS Business Resource Group, Horizon's DEI committee where we work towards ensuring equitable and inclusive planning and buying practices across minority-owned and targeted media partners, and Horizon's Limitless Communications committee, which was founded by Horizon's top female executives to empower and inspire employees by striking out the "N'T" inside women's heads and hearts—I am led to finding my purpose through my passion.

BIOGRAPHY

Edwina Morales is a second-generation Hispanic New York native and a graduate from St. John's University with a degree in marketing and international business.

She is an integrated advertising and marketing bilingual professional with thirteen years of strategic planning experience who is particularly interested in understanding human behavior and building brand relationships and experiences with consumers through this understanding.

Edwina transitioned her new role into the world of

multicultural media strategy and planning in 2018, and since then has been named a 2021 Adweek Media All-Star, 2021 Ad Age Media Planner of the Year Finalist, and a 2021 VAB Rising Star.

CESAR MORALES

"Con ganas, todo es posible."

Coming to the United States from Mexico at age six was a culture shock for me. My parents, my brother, and I came with little else besides the clothes on our backs. *Mi mamá* was a superstar accountant in Mexico. I'm sure she would have owned her own business by now. However, she chose to follow my dad in pursuit of the "American Dream." But that dream soon turned into a nightmare.

We did not speak the language, so my mom had trouble finding a job in her profession and cleaned restaurants instead. She was treated like a second-class citizen, or, as we were officially referred to then, an "illegal alien." Those words are so dehumanizing.

So many teachers mispronounced my name in school that I got used to it. But my third-grade teacher's belief in me changed my path. It was then that I realized my path to a better future was through education. I fought hard to learn English and before I knew it, I was making honor roll and receiving high marks from all my teachers.

I remember my mom celebrating any little achievement I ever had. Even if it was just a spelling test. She would place it on the fridge and tell me how great she thought I was. Eventually, I graduated in the top two percent of my high school and received a full-ride scholarship to college.

Once I began my professional career, I noticed that, far too often, Spanish-speaking people were treated differently in business settings. Whether as a customer or an employee, if our skin was not of fair complexion or we had a hint of an accent, we were deemed unintelligent or treated like our dollar didn't count. I remember many instances of my family receiving subpar customer service, and I couldn't help but think that it was because of our ethnicity.

Today, I work as a leader in serving Spanish-speaking customers. I created a bilingual unit, El Centro, within my organization, that has multiple layers of bilingual support. My goal is to make sure our people are being valued and seen through impeccable customer service. We focus on *la bienvenida*, to ensure our customers feel welcomed and valued. I want my team to treat our customers as I know they are, as we are, with dignity and respect, as valuable and worthy of our time. I will never forget when my mom wasn't treated that way. She deserved so much better.

Many don't realize the difficulties that they will face as they leave their home country in pursuit of a better life. There were moments of fear, days with hunger, but one thing I will never forget is feeling like I didn't belong. Every day, when I work with *nuestra gente,* I do it with my mom in mind.

BIOGRAPHY

Born in Orizaba, Veracruz, Mexico, Cesar Morales is an experienced bilingual Latino leader who believes the key to positive results is effective coaching. He has a proven record of driving results by focusing on the most important asset of any company, the people. He brings positive energy and promotes inclusive innovative work environments.

Cesar is also an award-winning public speaker and holds a Bachelor of Science in Business Management from the University of Phoenix and is an executive MBA candidate through Arizona State University.

MY JOURNEY AND PAYING IT
FORWARD

DR. EDWIN MOURIÑO

"So, my hope is to make a difference by paying it forward."

I began my life journey in New York City (NYC), born to a single mother who had the support of her family, my grandparents (the Ruiz family), who raised me. They sacrificed to ensure my brother and I attended Catholic school and received a solid education, hoping for a better future for us. They migrated from Yauco, Puerto Rico, looking for a better life in a strange land known as NYC.

From early on, I indicated that I wanted to be a doctor. Of course, this made my family proud, especially since no one in my family had a college education. A couple of years into college, I broke my grandmother's heart by dropping out of college and entering the Air Force. I promised her I'd return with my degree, which I did. I have a PhD, which makes me part of the one percent of the world of people with a PhD and probably the .0001% being a Latino PhD. So I did become a doctor, just a different type.

I share the above not with a bragging intention, but highlighting my humble beginnings. I'm similar to many Latino children today, with no real guide, since no one in my family had gone to college or the military. So, I was sort of on my own Juan Ponce DeLeon journey, discovering along the way in my life-long learning experience, most of the time with no or very few Latino role models.

My professional experience has been one that started in the US Air Force, and since then, I have worked extensively in the corporate setting in a variety of industries and roles. In the last almost twenty years, I have also worked in higher education, bringing my corporate experience into the classroom. Along the way, I have authored and presented on a variety of human capital topics and trends, several related to the Latino demographic.

I am particularly focused on the Latino aspect for a couple of reasons. One is obviously because I am Latino and have lived the Latino, bilingual, bicultural experience. Secondly, because I usually see the Latino take a background role to other demographics. I want to be part of the movement that educates others on the impact of the Latino demographic on society, work, and as a consumer.

In addition, I've tried along the way to pay it forward by speaking at local high schools and work to mentor Latino students, especially with so many Latinos who do not go to college for a variety of reasons. Recently, my mother passed away, right before Mother's Day. She along with my abuela helped shape the man I am today. They paid it forward for me, and today and tomorrow, I want to continue to mentor, speak, educate, and inspire other future

PhDs from our rich Latino community. So, my hope is to make a difference by paying it forward.

BIOGRAPHY

Dr. Edwin Mouriño is a USAF veteran, practitioner, educator, and author. He is the founder of Human Capital Organization Development (HCOD), and his focus is on helping leaders and organizations help themselves. His philosophy is one of helping others help themselves.

Dr. Mouriño also brings this philosophy to the classroom in helping students help themselves. He has mentored high school Latino students and spoken to many students about their future aspirations and education. Dr. Mouriño has spoken at numerous events on trends and the changing diversity with its benefits. He enjoys reading, movies, biking, and traveling with his wife.

ADRIANA OCAMPO SENIOR

"I would not be here today if it weren't for those countless women who blazed this trail for me. I am standing on the shoulders of giants."

I am an energetic and customer-focused leader with twenty-four years of experience in the aerospace industry.

I have been blessed to reach senior levels of leadership, technical achievements, and career wins at the Boeing Company, but what surpasses these many accomplishments is my giving spirit and tireless work through community service to others.

I am currently a member of the Boeing Global Services (BGS) Technical Operations Strategy team, where I help create high-value solutions for government, domestic, and international customers, including go-to-market strategic planning for priority proposals to demonstrate competitive ability and commitments to the US Department of Defense.

I was born and raised in Colombia, as the proud daughter of

an engineer father and Colombia's first female marine zoologist. My mother is my role model and a trailblazer. She epitomized unconditional love, but she also epitomized unconditional discipline. My Mom definitely taught me the importance of earning my way.

I completed elementary and high school at the Liceo Benalcázar, an all-girls private school in Cali, Colombia. From an early age, I developed a fascination with how things work and dreamed to study here in the United States.

After graduation, I went to British Columbia, Canada, to spend one year as an international exchange student. Then I returned to Colombia to begin my studies in industrial engineering at the Universidad del Norte in Barranquilla, where my parents reside. It was thanks to an exchange program offered by UniNorte, and the support of my parents, that I was able to make my dream of studying college in the US a reality.

The original plan was for me to spend only one semester in Missouri, but once I set foot on the beautiful Mizzou campus on that very cold January morning, I saw so many opportunities ahead of me, and decided to stay and complete my Bachelor's of Science in industrial engineering degree there. I also obtained a Master of Business Administration degree at Maryville University's John E. Simon School of Business in St. Louis, MO, and I began my career at Boeing in 1997.

Throughout my life, I have been very fortunate to have strong, female mentors and sponsors who challenge me every day to be great. It is not an overreach to say that those women gave me the courage to embrace my faith and confidence; and to refuse to allow challenges, doubters, or setbacks to have power in my life. I dreamed and worked my way through college in the US into the aerospace industry and through the ranks of leadership at The Boeing Company. I would not be here today if it weren't for those countless women who blazed this trail for me. I am standing on the shoulders of giants. Therefore, I would like to pave the way forward, and to attract and inspire more young Hispanic girls to get into STEM fields of studies. Now it is my turn to lift up the next generation of female Hispanic leaders. *Sí se puede!*

BIOGRAPHY

Adriana Ocampo Senior is a leader in the aerospace industry and a member of the Boeing Global Services' Technical Operations Strategy team. She serves on the national board of directors of the Society of Hispanic Professional Engineers.

Adriana was recently accepted into the DFW Hispanic 100 Latina Leaders organization and is a recipient of the Women of Color in Technology "Community Service in Industry Award."

Adriana was also the first Hispanic to be inducted into the University of Missouri's IMSE Hall of Fame, and this year she was appointed as a board member for that organization. Adriana holds a Bachelor of Science in Industrial Engineering from the University of Missouri and an MBA from Maryville University.

DIANA OCHOA-LORENTI

*"Empowerment is nothing other than recognizing our greatness
at its best, recognizing our own totality, knowing that we are not
missing anything, and we don't need anything else from outside;
we are enough, and everything that we need has been given to us.
If you don't promote yourself, no one will."*

At the early stage of my marketing career in Long Island, NY, I realized that I was in a competitive environment, primarily dominated by men, and if I wanted to stand out and have a successful career, I was going to have to do something different.

I decided to strategize and to identify my biggest strengths and weaknesses. I had a thick Latino accent in a primarily white environment, where sometimes I felt like a mole. After a careful analysis of my skills, I was able to clearly identify my unique value proposition (UVP), just like any other product! I was in my early twenties and new to the American culture, as well as to corporate

America, but I realized that amongst all my colleagues, I was the only bilingual marketer with a Latina cultural background, who understood the pain points and needs of one of their most desired target audience—the Hispanic population.

So, I rolled up my sleeves and tackled my new positioning. One of the biggest challenges that I had to face was my own limiting beliefs and insecurities. I was fortunate for the great colleagues and friends that I had by my side who empowered me and motivated me by recognizing my differences, as well as my own abilities and experiences.

I read numerous books and stayed up at night studying different acculturation levels and respective behaviors and needs. I attended as many industry conferences as possible. I had a long commute to the city every day, and I used that time to educate myself so my mind was always sharp and inspired to come up with new marketing initiatives.

I also joined Toastmasters to face my fear of public speaking. It was a great experience. I met amazing people and grew so much with that program. As I started seeing results in my career in terms of respect from senior management, being asked to participate in more meetings and colleagues interested in hearing more about my marketing recommendations as well as projections, I started building a solid trust in myself and therefore confidence. That also allowed me to remove those limiting beliefs and create new ones, where I was able to see myself achieving my career goals by embracing my uniqueness.

The dedication, hard work, and commitment to my self-growth paid off. I was recognized and promoted by my employer for my performance. However, the biggest lesson that I gained from that experience was that people can guide us and motivate us, but no one can tell us what we are best at. Only we are the experts of our own talents and story.

I also learned that empowerment is nothing other than recognizing our greatness at its best, recognizing our own totality, knowing that we are not missing anything and we don't need anything else from outside; we are enough, and everything that we need has been given to us. In this case, I just needed to be me, without a mask.

BIOGRAPHY

Diana Ochoa-Lorenti was born in Guayaquil, Ecuador. She is a marketer and a loving mother of two amazing kids. She has worked for major industry players, such as Nature's Bounty, Cablevision, Univision, NBCUniversal, and RCN Telecom, helping them improve market share and grow customer bases. In addition to her love for family and people development, Diana is passionate about her career, which has allowed her to build a successful trajectory over the past seventeen years in the telecommunications and media industry.

ACTION IS MY WAY

LINDAMARIA ORTEGA FRANCO

"Significant actions make substantial changes. But the sum of small actions can change the motion of everything. I consider myself a small action."

The most significant influence in my life is my parents. Both are first-generation with university degrees and both found their purpose in doing social and education work.

Everything started at a health center in a small town called San Pedro Ayampuc in Guatemala. My father was the doctor assigned and my mother, the social worker—it's the place where my parents met, so my life begins with social work.

One of my first memories is with my mother at one of her projects: people receiving literacy classes under a tree because of the lack of schools and infrastructure, in 1983. My father had his clinic at home. People used to come looking for the doctor and bring tortillas, chuchitos, and food, for the doctor who did not charge.

I often asked them about their jobs and why people were so

friendly to them. They always claim loyalty and solidarity as their mantra. They started a consultancy company in 1992, focusing on education and health, of course. I was thirteen years old. I helped them with every step, moving furniture and computers, setting up working environments, quotations, and everything possible.

I grew up in a family focused on education and social development and worked with my parents on some projects. One was with the European Union at eighteen, when I visited Madrid, Spain, for the first time. It was love at first sight.

After Hurricane Mitch, I helped with the creation of ACUDE, focusing on the recovery of the Chorti area in Guatemala. Then opportunity knocked at the door. We were able to do projects with international organizations and local governments. I got a scholarship and moved to Spain and started working on a project about immigration and integration through participation. That changed my plan and I stayed two more years.

I learned more about how to change the world with other projects focused on immigration, youth, and international education. After a while, the Vicente Ferrer Foundation, an organization that worked in India, hired me, which triggered many more changes.

After ten years in Spain working on projects in different parts of the world, the organization where I worked decided to open operations in the United States. They chose me for this endeavor. For me, it was the beginning of a new life—a Latina executive representing a Spanish organization in the US. It wasn't easy. I learned about philanthropy and nonprofit organizations in the US, of course. My background is international, and this was about locals.

After three years, I decided to take another leap of faith, reinvent myself, quit the foundation, and start my own project, "Red and Green Connection." But life always puts angels in your way, and I have collaborated in many others' initiatives targeting women, culture, and young people. So far, I have been a small piece on initiatives that change lives directly and indirectly for at least six million people.

BIOGRAPHY

Art and education are a big part of Lindamaria Ortega Franco's life. Although she has a business background, her knowledge of different disciplines allows her to improve the community and, hopefully, the world.

Her passion for continual learning, understanding, and education has driven her career and personal interests. She can be considered an artist and a social entrepreneur focused on initiatives that strive for economic, social, and cultural development, women's empowerment, and global citizenship.

Currently, she works at the IPMCS—Institute for Public Management and Community Services—and as a PhD candidate in public affairs at Florida International University.

TO THINK IN ENGLISH AND SPEAK IN SPANISH

NATHALIA ORTIZ

"Until the Hispanic community can learn to band together and uphold each other in all areas of life, we will never be able to effectively demand that non-Hispanics give us the respect and compensation we deserve. Period."

I was born and raised in the United States, of a Cuban mother and a Colombian father. Once I started school, English became my primary language. It's the language in which I think, yet, as I grew into an adult, I became borderline compulsive about translating every word into the language spoken at home: Spanish. Thus, code-switching became my superpower.

When I became a broadcast news reporter, being fully bilingual and bicultural served me well. Because of it, I was able to land jobs at local news stations owned by Univision, Telemundo, News 12, and NBC. But here's the reality: While most media companies I worked for seemed eager to hire bilingual journalists, few, if any, were willing to compensate us when we did double the work of our monolingual counterparts. And the ugly truth that many of us don't openly speak of is that sometimes the people in charge were Hispanic. The biggest tragedy is that we take advantage of ourselves.

In the beginning of my reporter chapter, I assumed that delivering English and Spanish-language live shots on the same day—sometimes during simultaneous newscasts—would be respected, even considered badass; or that shooting, writing, and editing the same special story twice (one for each language) would be greatly valued. Instead, most newsroom leaders did not give it a second thought; yet, it became an expectation that was not accompanied by a better position, a bonus, or a higher-than-average salary.

I thought that taking on double the responsibility of my monolingual peers was part of a long-term strategy that would eventually pay off—literally. But what I found in my experience and in speaking with other fully bilinguals in the industry is that many newsroom leaders treat us as though they are doing us a favor because they are "allowing" us to get double the exposure. Many rookie reporters take the bait, all for the chance to secure a solid footing in the industry. And for me, it did that; but once years passed, the added responsibility minus the proper remuneration became more of a burden than a source of prestige.

I am thankful for the opportunity God and all my hiring managers have given me. I would not be the journalist I am without them. Some of them have become mentors and sources of support. However, I would also be remiss not to point out the grievances sometimes inflicted by members of our own Hispanic community.

So, my message is this: As the largest minority in the US, it's imperative we learn that solidarity is not about enjoying each other's foods and celebrating each other's customs. It's about taking a stand for each other as humans, especially in the workplace. The skills that distinguish us from our peers add value to the organizations we work for. Until the Hispanic community can learn to band together instead of perpetuating our own exploitation, we will never be able to effectively demand that non-Hispanics give us the respect and compensation we deserve. Period.

BIOGRAPHY

Nathalia Ortiz is a bilingual journalist with experience in English and Spanish-language media. She has worked as a reporter and anchor at local news stations in South Florida and Greater New York City.

She created the Hispanic media department at the Diocese of Brooklyn and led the launch of a Spanish-language digital and print newspaper for the Catholic community in Brooklyn and Queens. She is also a contributor for NBC Latino and a host for Comcast Newsmakers in Florida and Washington, DC.

Nathalia recently launched Natush Media, a company that creates video content for English and Spanish-speaking digital audiences.

THE DREAM IS NOW

KEVIN ORTIZ

"The dream starts the moment you develop an aspiration. And I aspire to inspire and build the next generation of young leaders with a sueñito."

When I was twelve years old, I walked the hazardous Arizona desert searching for mi sueñito. When I share my story, I often neglect to share the vague memory I have of the day my father said goodbye to his wife and three kids searching for El Norte. I was five years old when that happened, and it feels like I am constantly reliving that moment. How hard it must have been for my mother and father—it is something that breaks me when I think about it. After seven years of separation, baseball games, and busy public bus rides without my father, the dream became a reality when we reunited with him in Orlando, Florida.

I went through high school as an undocumented student. It was clear that my dream (and my parents' dream) of a college education would become a dream deferred. After my 2008 Colonial High School graduation, I did not go to college. Then, in 2012, President Barack Obama announced a new policy called Deferred Action for Childhood Arrivals (DACA). DACA provides renewable, two-year protection from deportation, an employment authorization card, and new opportunities to pursue our dreams. For me, that meant attending college.

Inspired by my protected status, the timely passing of Florida's out-of-state tuition waiver for select high school students, and the National Scholarship from TheDream.US, I graduated cum laude from the University of Central Florida in 2017. My diploma now hangs in my parents' living room as a reflection of their hard work and sacrifice. It is the visual representation of the dream realized.

My story is not unique. It is a partition in the tapestry that is the immigrant experience, and it is far from encapsulating the complete undocumented narrative.

It has been my experience that having a clear path and confidence in life after college is uncommon among most college graduates. For undocumented college graduates, that lack of clarity and purpose multiplies. A college education is an impossible dream, and it is almost impossible to dream beyond an impossible dream— though we try.

The search for purpose led me to join Truist Leadership Institute as a student leadership fellow in 2018. I will never forget what a senior teammate shared with me during my first week of training. She called my role "the dream job." At the time, I was not sure what she truly meant.

But after three years of visiting colleges and universities from Penn State to Florida State, I know what she meant. The same kid who could not attend college now travels to colleges and universities across the United States, teaching leadership development.

It is now 2021 and the dream continues. This fall, I will begin my MBA at UNC-Chapel Hill, with a full fellowship and acceptance to the respected Vetter Dean's Fellowship program. My journey has taught me that the dream is now. The dream starts the moment you develop an aspiration. And I aspire to inspire and build the next generation of young leaders with a *sueñito*.

BIOGRAPHY

Kevin Ortiz is a senior student leadership specialist at Truist Leadership Institute, where he creates and delivers leadership development programming for college students using principles of neuropsychology. Kevin is an MBA Candidate at UNC Kenan-Flagler Business School and a graduate of The Dream Lead Institute fellowship.

Born in Mexico and raised in Florida, Kevin is an advocate for diversity, equity, and inclusion in Hispanic communities in the US, and he serves on multiple nonprofit boards supporting Hispanic and immigrant communities. Kevin is a graduate of the University of Central Florida and was recently recognized as *Triad Business Journal's* 20 in their 20s.

BLANCA ORTIZ-SKELDING

*"I made the choice to be myself, to embrace what makes me
uniquely me, because that's when I am my best."*

I am a first-generation American. My parents immigrated to
the United States from Guatemala and Mexico, and met in Los
Angeles, the "City of Angels" and "home of gang culture". Neither
of my parents have more than a sixth-grade education; they came
to the US in pursuit of the "American Dream," to give us kids the
opportunity at a better life.

I grew up in East LA and South-Central LA, alongside my two
younger siblings. My father was the breadwinner, and my mother
was a stay-at-home mom. Dad worked odd jobs from construction
to gardening, but money wasn't enough to support our family and
mom had to apply for government assistance. I can still remember
as a kid going to the grocery store with mom, food stamps and
vouchers in hand and loading our shopping cart with food from the

program-approved list, which unfortunately for me, didn't include Fruit Loops.

Spanish was the only language spoken at home, and I didn't learn to speak English until the third grade. From a young age, my parents were strict about my friends and ensured I didn't get caught up with *"cholos"* (gang members).

School was my number-one priority; I was expected to get good grades and to attend college. I was accepted early-admission to an engineering school in New Jersey. I was so excited I shared the news with my friends and teachers. One teacher, a white female, told me, "You do realize the only other Hispanics at that school will be the janitors?" I was stunned. I didn't know what to say.

I graduated, and three days later I left LA for Jersey. As it turned out, many of my classmates were also Hispanic/Latino. I wish I could've gone back and told her.

Getting through college wasn't easy. My parents were only able to help pay for my freshman year. After that, I had to rely on scholarships, money I saved from internships, and loans. One year I even had to ask my boyfriend (now husband of seventeen years) to co-sign a loan. In 2006, I graduated with a BS in chemical engineering. As I walked across that stage, I looked out and saw the pride in my parents' faces. I felt overwhelmed with emotion. I was the first in my family to not only graduate high school, but also to get a college degree.

Fast-forward fifteen years into my engineering career, and my success hasn't been without struggle. Like that teacher many years ago, I've run into many who've tried to put me down for who I am.

As a female Latina in a predominantly white, male-dominated field, I've been told, under the guise of "constructive" feedback, to be less direct, less assertive. For a time, I tried to behave differently. Eventually I realized everyone wants something different and conforming to others' opinions is a never-ending struggle. I made the choice to be myself, to embrace what makes me uniquely me, because that's when I am my best. So be yourself; success is waiting!

BIOGRAPHY

Blanca Ortiz-Skelding is a skilled process development engineer with more than fifteen years of professional experience in Fortune 500 companies (Johnson & Johnson, Campbell Soup, Mars, Kellogg's, and Pfizer). She currently co-leads the Pfizer Latino Community colleague resource group and leverages that platform to give back to the local community.

She also volunteers her time with organizations such as Communities in Schools of Kalamazoo (CIS) and Kalamazoo Regional Educational Service Agency (KRESA), to speak to K-12 students about her career path.

In 2021, Blanca was recognized by the Healthcare Businesswomen's Association (HBA) as a Rising Star for exemplifying leadership and having demonstrated noteworthy achievements in her career.

HARDSHIP AS ADVANTAGE

JESSICA PALACIOS

"Wear your hardship with pride."

When I reflect on the lessons I have learned over the years, those passed down from *mi mamá y mi tía* are the most poignant. These are lessons I never found in a book or a webinar—they were lessons learned by example. My main takeaway from these powerful Latinas is that it is never the end. Even if it feels that way in the moment, there is another chapter beginning on the other side of that deep, dark experience.

When my father passed away, my mom was twenty-three. And because she had come to America from Colombia at age sixteen, she had not yet completed her schooling. So, she took the skills she did have—speaking two languages and driving a car—and became an overnight courier.

When my aunt was a victim of gun violence in Colombia, she was twenty-one. As she lay on the pavement, wondering if it was the end, she prayed and sang to the angels by her side. When you talk to her to this day, she is grateful to be alive, even if it means being paralyzed.

As a young person living through these experiences, what I took away is that it is vitally important to be resilient in life. In an effort to imitate my role models, I learned to persevere in the face of challenges—and this, I have come to learn, has become my competitive advantage.

When I graduated from university, I never dreamed my first job would be in a warehouse. As the sole female employee in the freight department, I certainly learned plenty, but it was not without resilience.

When I started my first human resources job, I started off in a temporary operations role, due to my lack of subject matter expertise. But I networked my way into a full-time role and managed to get a master's at night to make up for lost time.

Once I had a taste for HR, I just knew it would become my career. It satisfied my insatiable need to help people, but with the added bonus of doing it at scale. HR enables a company's human capital infrastructure, so I knew that by pursuing a career in HR, I would get to be a human advocate every day.

These experiences became part of my identity, not just my career. And they set my experience at BlackRock up to be what it is today. Never have I worked for a firm so dedicated to the issues that matter most to me personally—climate, racial justice, financial inclusion. So, for me, being part of BlackRock's HR team is both a pleasure and a privilege. I feel incredibly lucky to contribute to BlackRock's purpose of helping more and more people experience financial well-being. And because of my upbringing as a first-generation Latina, I have the unique ability to empathize with those who have persevered through hardships to make their dreams come true.

So, my advice? Wear your hardship with pride. Do not allow naysayers to convince you that corporate America isn't the place for you. You belong here—and we need you.

BIOGRAPHY

Jessica Palacios is the Head of Diversity, Equity, and Inclusion (DEI) for talent acquisition at BlackRock. In this capacity, she leads a Center of Excellence established to drive and support DEI projects, partnerships, and practices on behalf of Talent Acquisition. In addition, Jessica leads Americas Campus Recruiting.

Outside of her professional responsibilities, Jessica also volunteers with the Association of Latino Professionals for America (ALPFA) and the Hispanic Scholarship Fund (HSF). Jessica holds a BA from Duke University and an MS in Human Resources from New York University. Jessica lives in the state of New York with her spouse and son.

GETTING IN THE GAME: AMBITION
OVER ADVERSITY

ANTHONY PARDO

"Don't let adversity prevent you from getting in the game."

As a young couple, my parents immigrated from Ecuador to the United States in the late 1960s, settling in Brooklyn, New York. My father dreamed of pursuing medicine here in the United States. But once here, he had to attend to more immediate concerns like learning English; as such, he had to pivot from his dream of becoming a doctor to a career that provided for his family.

He worked his way from clerical jobs while in night school, becoming a supervisor within the payroll department of one of New York's largest hospital systems. His tenacity provided a road map for me once I decided to pursue a career in baseball.

Though I grew up with many Ecuadorian traditions, and was raised in a bilingual home, I fell in love with America's pastime. I started in Little League at the age of seven and played baseball throughout my school years and into adulthood. My love of baseball inspired my choice of college and my course of study.

Being realistic, I did not believe I was going to make it to the majors, but I did think that I could pursue a career in sports journalism. As such, I went to St. John's University and pursued a bachelor's degree in journalism with a minor in sports management. Though I enjoyed my time at St. John's and loved my internships at local newspapers, I knew that I wanted to get closer to the game than reporting from the press box.

Just as my dad pivoted towards working in a hospital to remain close to his dream of medicine, I knew that to get close to the business of baseball, I had to be in the room where it happens: the Commissioner's Office at Major League Baseball (MLB). Despite having no connections to the league office, after months networking, I was fortunate to land a job in office operations, working in the mailroom, where I learned the ropes of the league from the ground up. In that role, I was able to meet a wide variety of people, which led me to my next position in the marketing department and later to the corporate sponsorship group. Almost fifteen years later, I am now director of account services, where I oversee day to day management of league, media, and club sponsorships, ranging from small companies to brands that are household names such as Budweiser, Gatorade, and Google.

As a first generation Latinx son of immigrants who is working for a storied American institution like MLB, I know how rare my story is, and I always pay it forward through the uplifting of the next generation of Latinx young professionals, whether as co-president of MLB's SOMOS, our Latinx business resource group, mentoring young Latinx professionals through organizations like

Prospanica, or as executive board member of the Vecinos Collective. Through my work for the Latinx community, I'm able to teach my dad's example to others: don't let adversity prevent you from getting in the game.

BIOGRAPHY

Anthony Pardo is the director of partnership activation at Major League Baseball, where he oversees day-to-day management for the league's corporate, media, and club partnerships. He has spent fifteen years in the organization, working his way up the corporate ladder after starting in office operations before moving into sponsorship.

Anthony also serves as the co-president of SOMOS, MLB's Latinx business resource group (BRG). He is an executive board member of the Vecinos Collective, a network dedicated to Latinx professional development and empowerment, and a professional mentor with Prospanica New York. Anthony is a graduate of St. John's University.

KARINA PAVONE

*"I was craving that secret sauce—the ability to connect with
people, their authenticity, and their vulnerability."*

Four people in a one-bedroom apartment on Miami Beach was not ideal, but it was all my parents could afford. It was 1981, and we had just arrived in the United States from Argentina with the clothes on our backs and their life savings of $1,000. I was nine years old, my sister was seven. We knew no one, we didn't speak English, and my parents' solution to help pay the rent was to sublet a cot in our living room to a nice man named Luis.

It wasn't easy, but we were pursuing the American Dream. There was no going back, even though my parents had purchased roundtrip tickets. Through the kindness of others, we found our footing. My mom made a friend whose daughter was my age, so I got all of her hand-me-downs. Luis helped however he could, even surprising us with small gifts like crayons and coloring books. Our building manager also watched out for us. Despite being young, I experienced and understood the value of community and helping others.

My parents often said, "We can't give you much, but we can give you an education." And they did. By working multiple jobs, they sent us to private schools. Although being the poor kid in a private school is not the same experience, it was at La Salle High School where I took my first psychology class. It was fantastic! This subject stimulated my intellect like nothing had before. When my teacher suggested that I start a peer counseling program, I was hooked. I knew helping people in this way was my calling.

In college, I was a mental health technician for the elderly and gravely ill patients. It was profound work—a privilege, really—and it made me appreciate humanity and the fragility of life. A few years after graduating with my doctorate in clinical psychology, 9/11 happened. Through an employee assistance program, I was able to help hundreds of people who were affected. Their stories were gut-wrenching. Overwhelming. And like my patients, I needed to heal from the experience.

I applied to Miami Dade College for a position that was outside my area of specialty, but I landed the job (and for that, I credit the well-crafted 'thank you' letter I sent after the interview). While I ascended the administrative ladder over the next sixteen years, I found myself missing the people connection. I was craving that secret sauce—the ability to connect with people, their authenticity, and their vulnerability. I didn't have a plan, but I knew it was time to find my place in the world again and help others.

In the spirit of giving back and making a difference in people's lives, I pursued a position with the nonprofit Amigos For Kids.

Three hundred applicants and eight interviews later, I was hired, and I know in my heart that it was meant to be. I now lead an organization that epitomizes my passion for helping children and families.

BIOGRAPHY

Karina Pavone is the executive director of Amigos For Kids, a nonprofit in Miami, FL, dedicated to preventing child abuse and neglect by valuing children, strengthening families, and educating communities.

She and her husband of twenty years are the parents of two young daughters, one with special needs. Karina received her Doctorate in Clinical Psychology (ABD) and her MS in Mental Health Counseling from Albizu University. She earned her BS in Psychology from Florida International University. Karina was the first in her family to graduate college and she still owns her first psychology book, *Psychology: A Way to Grow.*

LT. COL. LEONEL A. PEÑA

"Education and hard work were my tickets to success."

At an early age, I was a forward thinker. Even as a young boy, I spent countless hours pondering different careers and my eventual retirement. So, I always wondered what I was going to do with my life, how it would end up, and if I was going to make a difference in this world. I didn't know how everything was going to turn out, but I knew one thing for sure: However life played out, I did not want to fail. So, I soon realized that learning was the key; education and hard work were my tickets to success.

I can remember watching *GI Joe* as a child. It was one of my favorite shows. At the end of each episode, one of the characters would teach a quick life lesson and then close it out by saying, "And knowing is half the battle." I remembered this throughout my life, as it reinforced my desire for knowledge of all types. As I got older and life was getting tougher, I figured that it might be a good idea to start to learn a few more words of wisdom to help me along the way.

As best as I could, I would remember motivational sayings whenever I heard them. They would keep me inspired and energized. Some of the many words of wisdom included, "nothing is impossible," "if you can dream it, you can achieve it," "drive on," "keep learning," "don't stop," "try harder," "challenge yourself," "develop good habits," "surround yourself with people of good character," and "get out of your comfort zone."

I hoped that keeping these phrases in the front of my mind would help me. Luckily, I was right. There were times in high school and college when I didn't think I was going to make it. There was definitely some difficult material to learn and quite a few tough tests to study for. But I kept repeating the words of wisdom to myself to provide focus and self-motivation. I knew that if I was going to aim high, I had to have these qualities in abundance. I was determined to chart my own course, and words of wisdom were the fuel to keep me on the path to success.

Years later, after repeating those words of wisdom in my mind countless times, I found myself not only getting through higher education and multiple Army schools but earning the privilege to lead troops at The White House and throughout the National Capital Region in direct support of several US presidents, numerous visiting foreign Heads of State, and the military's most senior leaders.

My career has been a wild, busy, and crazy ride, but it has also been meaningful, eventful, and more fun than I could have possibly imagined. I still stock up on words of wisdom as I come across them. They still motivate me and remind me to keep learning, and that nothing is beyond reach.

BIOGRAPHY

Lieutenant Colonel Leonel A. Peña is an accomplished leader with over nineteen years of experience managing and directing successful Army units and organizations. He has led multiple groups in direct support of the nation's most senior leaders, visiting Heads of State and other foreign dignitaries, and events of national and international significance.

Lieutenant Colonel Peña holds master's and doctoral degrees, as well as a diploma from the US Army Command & General Staff College. He has been inducted into the Honorable Order of Kentucky Colonels and recognized by the Texas State Senate for his professional achievements.

TO DAYDREAM OR NOT TO DAYDREAM, THAT IS THE QUESTION

ROCÍO PEREZ

"The power of imagination can take us where we desire to go, regardless of the state of our current circumstances."

I am the daughter of Mexican immigrants who moved frequently from city to city in search of work. As a child, I could only imagine what success could be like amidst the adversity we lived in daily. At five, I was already daydreaming of becoming a teacher. Yet, growing up, my elementary school teachers and even my own family were telling me, "You will never make it." I was well on my way to making their predictions come true.

I had the choice to either live or die. At age twelve, I ran away from my hard-scrabble and abusive childhood. At fourteen, I got into an abusive relationship, quit school midway through seventh grade, and wound up pregnant. Still, inside I continued to dream and imagine a different future. I so desperately wanted out that I became emancipated and, with only a sixth-grade education, fought for the right to attend college and won.

My love for my son, Victor, inspired me to do whatever it took to keep him safe. At a devastating moment, having endured abuse, homelessness, and hunger, I swore to myself, "Never again!" I consciously chose to break the cycle of poverty, abuse, and limitation. The journey was arduous. I was in school Monday, Wednesday, and Friday, and worked at the University. On Tuesdays and Thursdays, I took the bus from one home to another, cleaning houses. Each day was a marathon, from getting up at 3 a.m. to get us ready for the day, taking the bus across town to the babysitter, back across town to school or work, and in reverse at the end of the day, falling into bed, often still dressed, around midnight. I put myself through college and earned a dual MBA while working full-time, building a home and, as a single parent, raising my son.

At age thirty-three, when I was on top of the world, I realized, "I've made it, and I'm still unfulfilled!" Within a year, I was diagnosed with a brain tumor. It was my past experience of imagining a different future that allowed me to overcome multiple barriers and hardships and put me on the path to wholeness. It was my understanding of the immense power of my own mind that changed my life. Once again, I daydreamed my way to success! It was then that I committed my life to helping others do the same.

From life's experience, even during the most difficult times of despair, I believe each of us has the capacity to "daydream our way to success." There is always another solution to a problem, as long as we use our imagination. The power of imagination can take us where we desire to go, regardless of the state of our current circumstances. Imagination can take anyone to a life of prosperity, empowerment, service, and happiness.

I've found that without daydreaming and expanding your imagination, you will get stuck. So, use your imagination and let your daydreams become your reality.

BIOGRAPHY

Rocío Perez is an unapologetic optimist and sought-after international speaker of truth. She has delivered hundreds of inspiring and life-changing leadership talks that have helped thousands of attendees embrace success by becoming more intentional. She believes everyone has the capacity to live an empowered life of prosperity, service, and happiness.

Rocío is the founder of Inventíva Consulting. She designed a seven-step coaching process and wrote an international best-selling book. Rocío recently created The MindShift Game to help people take more courageous, consistent actions, build their confidence, expand their vision, step into their power, and elevate their energy.

INSPIRATION & PERSPIRATION

FRED PHILLIPS

"Through inspiration and perspiration, immigrants and their children reach beyond limits to grasp dreams."

We are a nation of immigrants, people who, by definition, have the courage to travel to new lands to build a better life for themselves and their families, and in so doing to propel our nation higher. My mother was born in rural Mexico and was the first person in her family to graduate from university; neither of her parents completed high school.

To generate income to support her siblings, my mother moved to Houston, Texas, and worked as a nurse in the VA Hospital. After personal setbacks, my mother raised me alone, and my earliest memories are of our sleeping on the floor of a small, rented apartment as my mother labored to save money to buy our first bed.

My mother's example of hard work and sacrifice are the strongest influences on my development. Through good fortune, I earned a scholarship to attend an excellent high school, which provided me with the academic and social formation to build a better life. Being told there are no limits to what we can achieve with focus and persistence—and through the efforts of my mother and grandparents—I obtained degrees from Cornell, Oxford, and Yale Universities.

As a way of expressing my gratitude for the opportunities that our country provided our family, my first three jobs were in government: a law clerk to a federal judge, a lawyer in the Justice Department's Honors Program, and a Fulbright Scholar.

I then worked in the private sector as a lawyer, an investor, and an entrepreneur, developing and commercializing technology to promote financial wellness and inclusion. Our company, Investor Cash Management, has the backing of sophisticated investors including Visa, and our partners include trillion-dollar asset managers and leading wealth management firms.

The vast majority of our employees are first- and second-generation immigrants who have come from around the globe to develop and apply their talents. Diversity is not a component of our hiring policy; instead, we focus on hiring the best talent we can find, and the result is a gifted team of diverse individuals who together are greater than the sum of our parts.

There is nobility in the immigrant experience. Immigrants seek, strive, and succeed. Their collective efforts across the socio-economic spectrum drive our communities and our country forward. Through inspiration and perspiration, immigrants and their children reach beyond limits to grasp dreams. In so doing, they set examples of what can be achieved individually and collectively. I am proud of my family's history, just as I am humbled by the momentous contributions of all immigrants who have sacrificed for the collective good.

BIOGRAPHY

Fred Phillips was born and raised in Houston, TX and has degrees from Cornell, Oxford, and Yale Universities. He began his career as an attorney, working as a law clerk to the Chief Judge of the US Court of Appeals, and then in the honors program of the Justice Department, and finally as a financial services lawyer for an international law firm.

After a Fulbright Scholarship, he directed investments in financial technology companies for ABN AMRO and then The Carlyle Group, both global private equity funds. He is now the founder and CEO of Investor Cash Management.

BARBARA PUJOLS

*"When life gives you lemons, don't settle for a cup—go for the
entire jar of lemonade!"*

From the moment I was brought into this world, I was already
fighting for my life. My grand entrance was like a WWE fight,
except it was the real thing. Born at seven months, only six pounds,
I was small enough to fit in my father's palm. Every time my parents
recount my hospital stay, they remind me how much food I ate.
Even as a newborn baby, I was determined to figure a way out, to
make a vow to victory and live to see another day.

As a child, I was mostly quiet and reserved. Maybe it had
to do with the fact that I was "sensitive" to the way others joked
about my appearance or the way I rapped off beat to Eminem's
"Mockingbird" on my CD player. Eventually, I would come out of
my shell. I decided that I didn't want to be made fun of, bullied,
afraid, or crying all the time. I decided that I wanted to be happy,
make friends, and laugh more. Therefore, I began to raise my hand
for every question asked, upset Mr. Monteverde for trying to do his

job, and if you heard a witch's laugh as you walked down the hall, it was probably me.

Later in life, as a sophomore in college, it seemed as if I had forgotten what a wise ten-year-old me once learned: to take control of my life and do what makes me happy. Again, my life was everything I didn't want it to be. At twenty, I was voluntarily admitted to the psychiatric unit at Hackensack Medical. I was devastated, exhausted, and extremely disappointed in myself. Evidently, I was at what most would consider a "breaking" point, but I never lost hope. I never lost sight of the possibility that maybe, just maybe that breaking point could have turned into my "building" point.

During my hospital stay, I remembered who I was. I reevaluated every decision that led up to that point. And even though I felt defeated, I was determined to figure a way out. Jim Rohn said, "It is not about what happens to you that matters, but what you do in response to what happens to you that counts." Thankfully, what happened to me was exactly what I needed to propel me forward into the life I did want.

Today, I am a better person because rather than run from the challenges, I run towards them. When life gives you lemons, don't settle for a cup—go for the entire jar of lemonade! Modify it to your liking until you feel it's just right. Immerse yourself in the kind of life that continuously builds your character, uplifts your spirit, and brings peace to mind. Let my story not only be a testament to what I've endured and how I've overcome the challenges, let it also be a reminder to what you are capable of and what is possible for you when you decide to make a vow to victory.

BIOGRAPHY

Early in life, Barbara Pujols wondered why she was prohibited from using her voice to stand up for what she believed in. As a result, Barbara has made it her life's mission to use her voice and share her experiences with enough people to inspire and empower them to find their own voice.

Barbara is an avid reader and writer and a spoken word performer. She is fascinated by psychology and has committed to a life of continuous learning and personal growth. Barbara loves her daily walks with her dog, Rex, and she is the proud oldest sister of three.

CARINA QUINTANA

"Don't wait, take inspired action, and lighten someone else's life today."

On my last trip to Nicaragua, I made spontaneous decisions knowing that these were guided intuitions. I wanted to be present and feel guided, so I surrendered and took action on what I felt God wanted me to do.

While connecting with my friend Oralia, I sensed the opportunity to be of service. Her disabled grandson, Jose, was born with spina bifida, a birth defect where his spinal cord failed to develop properly. Because of multiple malformations, he also needed a permanent colostomy operation, but even with all of his health conditions, Jose remains such a happy boy. Jose must be bathed daily to avoid any type of infection.

For the past six years, Oralia had to purchase water daily from a neighbor and carry it home in buckets. These buckets are also what she uses to cook, bathe, and clean. At times she did not even have the money to purchase water, so they had to go without it, making it a stressful situation for Jose's health and his overall quality of life.

Oralia's situation broke my heart. "How can this be?" I asked myself. Without hesitation, I met up with Oralia and went to the water distribution center that day. I took care of the expenses to provide her and Jose with running water. Three days later, Oralia and Jose had running water in their residence, which meant she no longer needed to carry buckets of water.

God only knows why this situation was placed in front of me. Sometimes I ask myself, "How I can help more people and how I can make a bigger impact in the world?" I feel there is so much to do, but so little time, yet I continue to ask for guidance and take inspired action when I'm guided to do so. I also look for opportunities to help and to be of service in any way shape of form. This is what my heart calls me to do.

Life is beautiful, and it will present us with unexpected opportunities that we can embrace and chose to explore. If we would be more in-tune with our surroundings, be present in the moment, and explore the human potential of kindness and compassion, we certainly would make it a better world. I believe it all starts with inspired action.

As I continue to build my nonprofit organization to help those in need, I rely on this guided and inspired action that ultimately takes me to the people that need me most. Many believe that they need millions of dollars in order to help people in need, but this is not the case. It all starts with just one person, a person like Oralia, who now does not have to carry buckets of water every day, which will help relieve some of her everyday workload. So, with this, I say to you: Don't wait, take inspired action, and lighten someone else's load in life today.

BIOGRAPHY

Carina Quintana is a fifteen-year corporate executive that left the corporate world to follow her passion and establish her nonprofit, From The Heart Organization. As a philanthropist for the past seventeen years in United States and in Latin America, she has volunteered with organizations like La Isla Network and Tzu Chi Buddhist Foundation. She is passionate about transforming the world for the better through acts of kindness and compassion. She has helped feed and promote health and wellness programs in villages in Nicaragua and Mexico. She is a member of the "Latinas 100" community and a published co-author.

CHERYL QUINTANA LEADER

"The light of truth shall set us all free."

One fateful day on the back lot of 20th Century Fox, I embarked upon a journey into cinematic storytelling and its ultimate life-enhancing imaginings. As a Latina born in Phoenix, who later moved west to Hollywood, I was saturated with La La Land's theater of girls/women being projected from a very limited point of view, especially of Americans with diverse ancestry.

Since I was ten, I had always had this sense that if all our narratives only included "he, his, him, father/son" that there was something definitely gone awry, excluding 52% of us powerful beings birthed/birthing all beings on Mother Earth.

The only daughter (of four) of a mechanic and a waitress to ever graduate high school/college (UCLA), and a Chancellor's Marshall/first Latina gymnast, I felt honored to wave the "First Gen" banner! Although my sights were originally set on becoming a heart or eye surgeon, life had other plans and I graduated an English major with a women's studies specialization. Always an avid feminist, I alternatively set out to heal feelings and change our world's narrow viewpoint through my ventures into re-writing and re-imaging our stories on screen.

Back on the lot, it was my Chilean friend who informed me about Universal's Hispanic Film Project. I became one of two writers selected to direct their own 35mm film about their "Hispanic American" experience. Since I didn't really have one, growing up in a neighborhood of no color where it was forbidden to speak Spanish or even acknowledge my Mexican mother and dark-hued sisters, I went to the library and discovered the Aztec's Calendar Stone legend.

Lo and behold, there was the Goddess of the Fourth Sun, who had been chosen to shine. The story involves the Black God of Night, who was deeply jealous of her and tortured her with claims that she did not get this job because she was qualified. No. She was chosen because of her beauty. Infuriated, she began to cry uncontrollably. And, being the Goddess of Water, her tears led to a great flood, which tragically ended her three and half centuries reign.

Having not known anything about my mother "Lynn's" Mexican family until I was thirty, it was revealed that she, a third-generation American, had grown up in Texas to signs that enforced "No Negroes, no dogs, no Mexicans, no Jews," with seven siblings (and not as an only child, originally claimed), and that my father could not and did not marry her because his family in Boston said he wasn't allowed to be with a Mexican, especially if she wasn't Jewish. (Later DNA results proved her maternal Dominguez line arrived in 1616.)

In the image of this Aztec Goddess myth, I unveiled my mother, whose real name is Maria de la Luz. Luz. The light. Thus, *Tanto Tiempo* (first words to the song *"Sabor a Mi"*) pays tribute to all mothers, who are beautiful enough to have children with, yet not allowed to share nor be proud of who she is, share her language or culture with her children or country. The light of truth shall set us all free.

BIOGRAPHY

Award-winning writer/producer/director, Cheryl Quintana Leader is one of the first Latinas ever chosen for Universal's Hispanic Film Project. Her semi-autobiographical 35mm film, *Tanto Tiempo*, won five National Awards, an induction into the MOMA/NY's Xicano Retrospective Archives, and she became the first-ever Latina to produce a US television hour-long special written by and about Hispanics in America (hosted by Edward James Olmos).

Her company, INDIVISION2000 Productions, is proud to have created dozens of educational media and live events in English/Spanish for the Latina/o community via casting/crewing diverse women in front of and behind the camera for over twenty years.

THE JOURNEY TO OPPORTUNITIES

DR. AZUCENA QUISPE

"Dreams come true; just believe in yourself."

My story starts in a port on the Pacific Ocean in Peru. We didn't have much, but enough to keep going. When my parents decided to move for better opportunities, I was sad and angry; I didn't want to leave my friends and the ocean I felt so close to. I didn't understand why, for little did I know that it was difficult for them too; but we were growing, and they were looking to give us a better future.

That's the way we are; our families made a lot of sacrifices to be in the place we are now. It is like it is printed in our DNA, telling us, "You are responsible for the next generation, and must open the way."

I was fortunate to have parents that believed education was the door to opportunities. My dad lost his dad when he was a child and started working to help his family and little siblings. He didn't have the opportunity to go to school, but when he met my mom, she helped him and graduated. This opened opportunities for him; later he continued his studies and graduated as an automotive electrician technician.

On the other side, my mother was the first person to go to college in her family; she didn't graduate because she started a family, and it was difficult with two little kids at home, but she always encouraged us to do our best and be good students.

I was privileged to live with these two wonderful role models and be a witness of their journeys and struggles as parents, to ensure we, their children, are better and have the opportunities they never had. It's then when I promised myself to get the highest level of education possible and open the way for my younger brothers. This was my dream.

When it was time to go to college, my parents didn't have enough money to pay it, but they were able to support me, and I graduated as an information systems technician. After some time working, I decided to go to college while working full-time.

A few years later, I graduated as a systems engineer and thought my life would change, but unfortunately, it was not like that. The shortages and lack of employment in the country were difficult; I was working two jobs and barely making it; however, deep in my heart, I knew this was not how it supposed to be.

What about my dream? Are dreams things you long for but never come true? What happens when the country's surroundings are telling you it's not possible, it's not going to happen, and not in this life? That's when you have two options: give up or have faith and believe this dream has a possibility. I guess I chose the second option. Some time later, an opportunity opened to come to the United States, and after two master's degrees and a doctorate, I can say now that dreams come true; just believe in yourself.

BIOGRAPHY

Dr. Azucena Quispe is currently a risk manager at a Global IT Retail organization. She has extensive experience in internal controls and compliance matters in information security and access management environments. Her research interests include information systems security, and implementation of compliance management solutions, policies, and procedures.

Dr. Quispe has an accomplished academic background receiving a bachelor's degree in systems engineering and holding two master's degrees in business administration and project management. She received a Doctorate in Information Technology with a specialization in Information Assurance and Cybersecurity in 2018. Also, she is associated with PMI, ISACA, InfraGard, and holds a certification as a Certified Fraud Examiner.

MAGGIE RIVERA-TUMA

"I am the true definition of an ordinary person with an extraordinary destiny."

I see my reflection every morning as I get ready for work. I barely recognize that once nine-year-old Puerto Rican girl who had a fast-food beverage thrown at her just for singing in Spanish as I walked down the street. "This is America; speak English," he yelled as he drove by, leaving me stunned and pondering what I had done to deserve this attack. As if being chronically homeless and rejected by society wasn't enough, layering on racism exasperated anxieties and elevated my childhood trauma.

As a homeless child, the trauma endured made it difficult to lead a healthy and stable life. I suffered physically, psychologically, socially, academically, and behaviorally. The true saving grace was when I was sent to live with my Abuela. Unfortunately for her, she inherited my twelve-year-old self and my rebellious behavior.

However, the foundation of love and guidance that she laid for me molded me into the woman I am today. When I was seventeen, Abuela passed, leaving me homeless again. However, this time, I was more equipped to fend for myself. Living on my own, I juggled work and high school. At age eighteen, I got a job at a bank. I worked hard to gain ongoing promotions throughout the years. In this field of work, I learned early on that if I wanted to succeed, I would have to assimilate. I had to modify my appearance, body language, and communication skills to fit their definition of executive presence. I had to suppress my authenticity to fit in the industry box, if I wanted to continue to grow in my career, or so I thought.

I found myself in a position that enabled me to both follow my passion and career goals when I started working in community development. In this role, I worked with many low- to moderate-income communities to promote economic development. I found myself in rooms with brilliant leaders who had the best of intentions but were not fully connected with what a day in the life really was like living in poverty. I found myself uniquely positioned to add value and create tangible impacts that changed the lives of many.

This impact did not go unnoticed, for I was tapped to join the Diversity, Equity, and Inclusion (DEI) efforts of my organization. I was asked to help tackle the challenges that plagued the inequitable culture of the banking industry. To impact the lives of those forced to assimilate, passed over for promotions, or those who were victims of unconscious biases.

I may have been that upset nine-year-old, confused by one

man's hate for the color of my skin. I might have been on the brink of giving up hope and being a statistic of the streets. However, I'm none of that. I'm Magdaline Maria Eloina Rivera-Tuma. I'm a mother of two, a wife, and an unapologetic, proud Latina, carving paths to promote authenticity. I am the voice for the voiceless. I am the true definition of an ordinary person with an extraordinary destiny.

BIOGRAPHY

Maggie Rivera-Tuma is the Hispanic, military, and veteran segmentation strategy manager at US Bank, leading the company-wide strategy efforts in Diversity, Equity, and Inclusion (DEI). Maggie has twenty-one years of experience in the banking industry with experiences ranging from retail, business banking, community development, and DEI.

Maggie serves as president of the board for the Hispanic Business Economic Development Center, vice president of New Sunrise Properties, and program committee chair for CHN Housing Partners. In addition to these leadership roles, Maggie also serves on The Hispanic Roundtable, the Cleveland Council of World Affairs, and the Lorain County Chamber of Commerce.

LIFE WITHOUT FEAR IS THE ONLY LIFE WORTH LIVING

CHRISTIAN J. RODARTE

"In life you only ever have two choices—fear or love. Will you lean into fear and be hardened, or will you lean into love and be softened?"

About two years ago, my life was turned upside down in the blink of an eye. In the summer of 2018, my younger sister was diagnosed with leukemia. Specialists and expert oncologists described the road ahead and what the chances were. With the odds stacked against us, she started an aggressive chemo protocol. Day-by-day, sometimes hour-by-hour, was the name of this game, one which required the utmost patience, understanding, and empathy. My vibrant, sassy, free-spirited, twenty-something sister was fighting for her life with so much grace.

She spent four and a half months in the hospital, and I was privileged enough to be by her side each day, often taking shifts with other friends or family. She got to see me work while I helped her get around the room and take walks along the oncology floor, where she had gotten to know other patients. Not a day went by that we wouldn't hear the chilling sound of the code blue alarm, often indicating someone was passing over—at that moment you pray that it's never you.

By November, while she was in full remission from the cancer, her body, just as explained by the oncology team, had taken a beating. On November 13, 2018, I was finishing up my daytime shift with her before our dad came for the evening. As I was walking out, she said to me, "Don't be late tomorrow, and don't forget my cherry Coke." I laughed, told her that I loved her and went home. The following morning just before 7 a.m., her oncologist called me to tell me she died. Her heart and lungs gave out, and there was nothing else they could do.

Frozen by the shock, I then had to call my parents and tell them their child had died. Everything was happening so fast, yet it felt like it was slow motion. It was a few weeks before we could lay her to rest.

It's now been over two years since she passed, but those four plus months we spent together in the hospital taught me that in life you only ever have two choices—fear or love. Will you lean into fear and be hardened, or will you lean into love and be softened? It would have been very easy to become hardened and angry at the world, but I knew she would not want me to be angry or sad, so I chose—because it is a choice—love. Every choice we ever make is a direct reflection of what we are choosing to lean into—fear or love.

The job we feel we're underqualified for, the commitment

we're scared to make, the business we're unsure to start, it all comes down to choosing fear or love. Life without fear is indeed the only life worth living, but you must always choose love.

BIOGRAPHY

Christian J. Rodarte, a third-generation entrepreneur, is founder and managing director of Autobiography, a dynamic communications consultancy with offices in Los Angeles and Miami.

His life's purpose is to create, amplify, and scale change. A humanitarian at heart, there is nothing more beautiful to him than seeing people shine in their power; when you shine, you give others the permission to do the same. He is relentlessly committed to making the world a better place. A native Angeleno, Miami is now his home.

UNDERSTANDING DIFFERENCES HELPS ACHIEVE SYNERGY ON THE JOB

STELLA RODRIGUEZ

"We all come from a variety of backgrounds and experiences; these differences should always be valued, so we need to be transparent about them and keep an open mind to understand each other better."

Starting a new job fresh out of college is a unique experience. You are full of excitement and ambitions, countered by the nervousness and apprehension that come with new beginnings. Many factors can easily make or break this opportunity, so keeping an open mind is crucial to have a positive memory.

My first full-time job was in a business that has been mainly dominated by men. In this position, I was paired to work with another person and, even though we had different titles and responsibilities, we needed each other to complete our work. My first assignment was what my peers liked to call an "opportunity" project—one that is significantly big in scope and being observed by various departments and executives. However, as a newbie, I did not have a clear understanding of the meaning of this so-called opportunity project. I just wanted to learn, grow, do a good job, and contribute to the growth of the business.

To start my project, I scheduled a jobsite visit with my co-worker to have a better understanding of the scope of work and develop a plan. We walked the entire area, took pictures, took measurements, and discussed ideas. Everything was going very well. The moment we were getting ready to leave the location, my co-worker made a comment that I never thought I would hear. He let me know how he classified himself in society followed by, "I have never had to work for a woman that is younger than me, much less one that is Hispanic."

In that moment, I just had a rush of thoughts. I barely knew this person, and I was already feeling there was an invisible line being drawn between us. However, I knew I needed to be honest with my co-worker, to break that barrier that I felt was being built.

I said to him, "I understand. However, I do not think you are working for me but working with me. We are a team, and we are working together because we need each other to complete our assignments. I believe they paired you to work with me because they understand you are a very experienced person, and I am just the rookie. I look forward to work with and learn from you." After this conversation, we carried on and we were able to successfully complete many assignments together until I moved to a different role.

Even though his choice of words may have not been the correct one, I did appreciate the openness to express his thoughts and listen to my response. We all come from a variety of backgrounds and experiences; these differences should always be valued, so we need to be transparent about them and keep an open mind to understand each other better. This encounter on my first big project at my first full-time job not only helped my co-worker grow, but also helped me grow. For that, I am thankful.

BIOGRAPHY

Stella Rodriguez serves as Mississippi Power's substation supervisor. She is responsible for the substation construction program, engineering, and construction, including capital budget goals. Rodriguez joined Mississippi Power in 2018, after working for Gulf Power and Southern Company Services in Georgia.

A native of Aibonito, Puerto Rico, she holds a Bachelor's degree in Mechanical Engineering from University of Puerto Rico–Mayagüez.

Rodriguez's major organization involvement includes co-founding Gulf Power Hispanic Network, and a Mamie K. Taylor Service Award (2015) for her commitment to the community through Citizens of Georgia Power–Forest Park.

THE PLAYGROUND SLIDE

ADRIANA ROSALES

"Sometimes children perceive things that cannot be verbalized. Children tend to see the underlying truth of reality."

As a first-generation Latina growing up in the United States, I was told that because I was American, I could achieve and have anything I wanted. Imagine being showered with daily reminders of how fortunate I was to be walking in the land of immigrants. Deep down inside, I longed to believe it was true. But as I got older, I felt and saw something completely different. I was surrounded by a system in a country that was not open to accepting someone like me.

As a young child, attending school with children that did not look like me who spoke a language I did not understand depleted my self-worth and confidence. At a very real and emotional level, I understood the story of America did not include me or people that looked like me. I was reluctant to admit it, but it was the truth. Sometimes children perceive things that cannot be verbalized. Children tend to see the underlying truth of reality.

In fifth grade, I remember being bullied by a white girl because I did not speak English like the rest of the kids. She, along with her entourage, would pin me up to a wall and then spit in my face and pull my hair because I was different.

My most vivid memory in elementary school was seeing one of the only Black kids in school bullied and harassed. During recess she ran towards the playground to hide under the slide, because the kids were throwing sand in her face. When I saw this happening, I ran to her and accompanied her under the slide. I told her that it would be ok, and that maybe we could be friends. To me this young girl was not Black. In fact, I did not understand color at the time. What I saw was that she was afraid. To me she looked just like me, a terrified kid trying to understand all the hate in the world.

When I was a young adult, I came to understand that this type of hate is something that is taught and that it runs deep in the many layers of American culture and makeup of this country. It cannot be negated as unreal or imagined.

My job as an American writer is to place you as witness under that playground slide. If I can do that, then I've done my job. The privilege of being American is not living the dream of getting what you want; rather, to remind others that it is possible to dream. Every day I'm grateful for the words that pour out of my heart in search of your heart. As a writer, I'm in search of people still hiding out under that playground slide, waiting to be embraced and told it's going to be ok; hate is not forever, and in America, love always wins.

BIOGRAPHY

Adriana Rosales is a seven-time author, featured as one of Forbes' expert panelists and a Forbes Coach Council member. She is a John Maxwell Certified Speaker, and a HeartMath® Coach. Her books have been translated into several languages. She continues to inspire women to write their personal stories in her yearly Latinas 100 project. An accomplished military veteran, she brings her background and years of experience navigating the corporate ladder to the front lines in her book, *Corporate Code, A Bottom-Up Perspective on Great Leadership.*

WHEN LIFE GIVES YOU LEMONS, WE MAKE LEMONADE

ANDRES RUZO

"Faith in the future is power in the present."

Life is difficult—change is difficult, and most people have always been afraid of change, sometimes freezing in their tracks, fearful of the unknown. In my case, I have always opted to embrace change, and now I do it with alacrity.

In 2007, after six years of losses, I found myself in a stressful situation with $3 million in debt, trying to discern whether I should quit and close LinkAmerica or keep grinding with faith and hope into the future. I called those seven years the "skinny cows," forgoing my salary for almost a year, letting go of over one hundred employees, and staying alive with only five employees. I knew that there was not a lot of time left and I had to make the decision quickly.

The next morning, I woke up to find my four children having breakfast when I knew that there was more to be done, and bankruptcy was not an option. I was ready for a full business transformation; change would drive a blessing that would make me stronger. Transformation demanded a drastic decision to sell all my manufacturing assets and buildings, to buy time to co-create a runway of opportunities in other directions.

By the end of the seventh year and after many sleepless nights, I drove towards certainty by implementing a new business model and services transformation plan. Faith in the future is power in the present—this was my mantra!

Once again, I was able to positively adapt and transform my life and my company. I focused on building strong and sustainable bridges with my clients and employees, providing them with high impact, high-value services rather than hardware sales. The change came with sacrifice and the ability to let go—and to let it FLOW!

By 2012, the company was being recognized nationally as the number-one fastest Hispanic growing business, with over $200 million in revenue—that in itself was an achievement that in 2007 seemed far-fetched.

I called those next seven years the "seven years of holy cows!" The resilience and persistence of adapting to change by being vulnerable and open to transformation was a critical path to continue my growth.

Today, I am intentional in everything I think, say, and do. Everything I do is purpose driven and drives positive disruption and welcomes change—with alacrity!

Finally, when life gives us lemons, we make great lemonade… and more—margaritas, pisco sours, Key lime pies, lemon bundt cakes, and much more. Let's welcome change with ALACRITY!

BIOGRAPHY

Andres Ruzo is the co-founder and CEO of LinkAmerica, a leading telecommunication, technology services company in the United States. He was born in Lima, Peru, in 1961, and moved to the United States in 1980 to pursue a degree in engineering at Texas A&M University.

As a successful entrepreneur, Andres has invested in over thirty companies in the IT sector. Outside of business, Andres is an active member of multiple organizations focused on serving the community. The motto he lives by and advocates is: "Choose your faith and live it daily, aligning your thoughts, words, and actions around it."

IVAN SALAZAR

"I strive to be decisive, courageous, and willing to always go the extra mile to help someone in need. I believe this mindset has allowed me to become an important fixture at my workplace and helped me literally save lives in the process."

I never shy away from a challenge, and this choice has meant that, as director of outlets for the Wyndham Grand Clearwater Beach, I've been forced to come up with creative solutions on the fly or make split-second decisions that could save lives. In just the last two years, I've had to jump into swift action in life-threatening situations not only once, but three times.

The first of these incidents occurred in 2019, when a guest who was dining in our restaurant started choking on his food. I was summoned to the restaurant and acted immediately, without thinking, and administered the Heimlich maneuver. I stood behind him and pressed his diaphragm, and was relieved when he expelled the bit of food from his throat. The guest and his family were very thankful and the experience created a bond between us. To this day, we are still in touch.

About six months later, a young child who was at the pool with his older siblings went for a swim and found himself at the deep end, unable to keep himself afloat. I was walking by the pool at the time, doing my rounds, and heard someone yell out that a kid might be drowning. Without hesitation, I jumped in the pool, not wasting a second to remove any of the items I was wearing. I pulled the kid out of the water and administered CPR, and soon enough, he was breathing again. The child's parents were called to the pool by his older siblings. They were so grateful, they cried and hugged me. Their kid was safe.

The third incident happened in 2020. A four-year-old child was at the pool with his parents. One of them stood up and went to retrieve something from their room, while the other one fell asleep. Meanwhile, the boy went into the pool by himself and, as he went further in, he became completely submerged in the water. A few people noticed that the child was not coming back up and someone called out for help. I saw the commotion from the restaurant and ran outside to help as he was pulled from the pool.

I quickly asked one of my team members to call 911, and rushed over to administer CPR. Thankfully, it worked. He slowly regained consciousness and became more responsive. By the time the paramedics arrived, he was fully conscious and everyone was so relieved. Some people began to applaud.

I aim to be the best version of myself every day of my life, both at work and at home. I strive to be decisive, courageous, and willing to always go the extra mile to help someone in need. I believe this mindset has allowed me to become an important fixture at my workplace and helped me literally save lives in the process. These incidents have not only left a huge mark on my life, but have also allowed me to leave a positive impact on the lives of others.

BIOGRAPHY

Ivan Salazar is the director of outlets at the Wyndham Grand Clearwater in Florida, a part of Wyndham Hotels & Resorts, the world's largest hotel franchising company. In his role, Ivan is involved in all aspects of the food and beverage operation.

Prior to Wyndham, Ivan spent thirteen years with Starwood Hotels & Resorts, where he held various food and beverage roles.

He grew up in San Diego, California, where he served as a mentor in his community as part of a big brother program. Ivan's passion for hospitality has taken him on a journey that included destinations such as the Hawaiian Islands and the mountains of Colorado.

BY HELPING OTHERS RISE, WE RISE!

JOHANNA SALAZAR

"To this day, I never let my humble beginnings get in the way. Instead, I always look for ways to give back and pay it forward."

When I was sixteen years old, I was a professional Hamptons cleaning lady. I even had my own housecleaning business. This was the beginning of my entrepreneurial life.

One day, my mother called and told me to help her clean for a few hours because the house she was cleaning was large and full of dust from all the construction going on. She literally said to me, "Don't worry, just come and help me, it won't be too much work, and it will be good money." That was all I had to hear. Being a cleaning lady was a normal profession in

my family, and it was starting to become my next career move.

At the time, I already had two jobs: food runner and marina store clerk/boat docking assistant. I was driven by challenge and achievement, so I was always looking for my next opportunity. This is also why I had a second job as a marina clerk and boat docking assistant; it kept me learning and experiencing new things. My mom also got me this job. She knew I was a good, responsible, and reliable worker, and I always made her look good.

The day came when she told me to go help her clean the large house with all the dust. She knew I would never say no to her. The house was gorgeous and the construction guys were super handsome. I was doing an exceptional job that day; for some reason, dust didn't bother me—even my allergies were okay for me.

Needless to say, I did such a great job, I left the day with a job offer from the owner's wife, Dawna. She asked if I would be interested in cleaning her home all summer. Without hesitation I said, "YES!"

That summer I juggled my three jobs as best as I could. I learned how to start a business (informally), I hired my first assistant, and I also met the man that would change my life forever, Fred. The owners of the large home, Fred and Dawna, gave me work for the next seven years, saw me grow up, and helped me land my first internship at MTV.

Fred became like the father I never had. He mentored me once a week after I finished cleaning and taught me the principles of entrepreneurship. I had no idea that I was learning so much, and that his teachings would impact me for the rest of my life. My curiosity and my determination drove me to listen with intent and ask lots of questions. He encouraged me to think big!

To this day, I never let my humble beginnings get in the way.

Instead, I always look for ways to give back and pay it forward. I love telling the story of when I used to clean houses, because this is a typical story for a lot of young Latinas. By helping others rise, we rise!

BIOGRAPHY

Johanna Salazar is a TV executive and tech entrepreneur focused on solving problems in education, food, and media.

UNSTOPPABLE

MARIA SALCEDO

"I am convinced that Hispanics are individually strong, but together and collectively we are UNSTOPPABLE."

Impactful ideas are not necessarily big and may come from where we least expect them. I learned this at an early age in Bogotá, Colombia, during my first corporate job as an intern at a large personal care products manufacturer. Since I was studying industrial engineering, I was asked to review a soap packaging line and identify potential improvements.

The process was very manual and tedious. Soap bars would come out of the manufacturing line and onto a conveyor belt, which would deposit the bars in large boxes. The boxes were then taken by individual laborers, who had to separate the bars by hand. The bars would stick together as they were coming out warm from the production line. As I was observing and taking notes, applying a time and motion study approximation, one of the female employees approached me. She said, "You know, all we need is for the soap bars to cool down before they are dropped in the box; that way they won't stick together, and that will save us a lot of time and effort." She was absolutely right; in that moment, she had given me the solution. I proposed to add a loop to the conveyer belt so that the bars would be allowed to cool down. The solve was extremely successful, and the employee and I were recognized multiple times for the improvements made to the process.

I have taken this experience with me, and it has shaped my professional career. After graduating with a degree in industrial engineering, I worked in finance for a credit rating agency. In this setting, I once again found that individual thinking is strong, but collective thinking is even stronger.

In 2006, I moved to the United States to further my education and pursue an MBA. For the first time in my career, I became aware of my role as a Hispanic professional in America. I was clearly a minority from an ethnic and gender perspective; yet, I never doubted my ability to create value and to do that with the support of my community in this new country. As a consultant, I was able to advise Latin American companies on how to enter the American market. In this setting, being bilingual and bicultural was an invaluable asset. Furthermore, as a team member at PepsiCo, I once again was able to leverage my experiences to support the growth of the Hispanic product offering, and bring ideas from the Latin American

business to the United States.

I feel fortunate to be able to see my upbringing as a differentiator and asset within this environment. In my current role as senior vice president of merchandising at Ulta Beauty, I am proud to represent Hispanic talent in the beauty industry, and help future leaders see their possibilities. I am convinced that Hispanics are individually strong, but together and collectively, we are UNSTOPPABLE.

BIOGRAPHY

With broad business experience across multiple industries and functions, Maria Salcedo is known for being a high-impact change agent and a thought leader. Maria has spent the last five years of her career at Ulta Beauty, where she is now the SVP of merchandising cosmetics and nails. She also worked for PepsiCo in various roles, and for McKinsey as a consultant.

She is originally from Colombia and has been living in the US for fifteen years. Maria holds an MBA from The Wharton School, University of Pennsylvania, and a BS in Industrial Engineering from Universidad de Los Andes.

ALL IT TAKES IS ONE

JENNIFER SANCHEZ

"Sometimes all it takes is for one person to believe in you."

Everything I ever accomplished required just one person to believe in me, even if it was only me at that moment. Also, it doesn't necessarily have to be the same person every single time. It can be one person placed at a given, specific time, with an assignment in my life for a specific season. They believed in me, which helped me rise higher and push harder towards my goals.

Sometimes, all it takes is for one person to believe in you. And in many cases, that is all that we will ever get. You never know who you are inspiring because you believed in them.

That is why I created a community for women—and this is our main focus. It's about believing in each other and creating a safe space for one another. In our society, life gets too busy for people to pay attention to each other. Many of us are so focused on our career, education, and family that we fail to focus on ourselves or vice versa. There is nothing wrong with concentrating on family, but life can become routine.

My father would tell me that I am so strong because I looked fine to everyone, although the struggle was real. I remember visiting my husband in prison monthly to keep him encouraged. I kept reminding him that we had God's favor in our lives, and that he would come home soon. I won't ever forget the moment that my husband came back after being incarcerated for two years, while my firstborn was still small. Once I passed that painful season, I knew it was time to fill someone else's cup.

I worked very hard to keep faith alive in our home. There were times that I had to put a smile on my face, so that everyone around me could feel "mommy got it together, so we are going to be okay." There was a time that I was so tired, discouraged, and depressed that I didn't even want to throw out the trash. I allowed it to stack up in a mountain of garbage, quite literally.

But while my husband was incarcerated, I learned two things: that it's hard as hell being a single mom, and that I needed to encourage others when they are struggling. Once it was over, I felt God tell me it was time to share all my knowledge with others.

So, my goal was to offer myself to one woman. After I told her my story, I said, "I want to coach you for free." She agreed. From that moment on, she learned in weeks what it took me years to figure out. She told me that I needed to launch my coaching business and start my workshops. We never looked back.

It only took one person during that time to say yes, this works, and the rest was history. Since then, we have grown a large network of women who support and encourage one another. We have made a difference in so many women's lives. Finding the right community to encourage you is essential if you have dreams and goals

BIOGRAPHY

Jennifer Sanchez is a big believer that women can have it all. She is the president and founder of The Women's Institute of Self Development and Efficacy (WISE). She recognizes the need to empower and provide a supportive environment for women. Jennifer has researched and created workshops, coaching programs, and motivational talks not only to help women transform their lives but to enhance their existing ones.

She is a contributing author in *Today's Inspired Latina, Volume 4*. Most recently, she was recognized on the Latinos 40 Under 40 list by *Negocios Now*. Jennifer resides in the northwest suburbs of Chicago with her husband and three daughters.

EVERY CHALLENGE IS AN OPPORTUNITY TO SUCCEED: HOW I DID IT

MONICA SÁNCHEZ FARFÁN

"Your story may be similar or totally different, but my advice is not to see challenges as obstacles. Look at them as an opportunity to learn and to test your ability."

Let me introduce myself. My name is Monica Sánchez Farfán-Mundis, and I'm a Peruvian living the life in the wonderful, sales-tax-free Delaware! I was born and raised in Lima, Peru, by my mother, Norka, a professional model—and the sweetest and most dedicated mom you could ask for—and my father, Pedro Ernesto, a larger-than-life personality who was a journalist/author, working seven days a week to give my sister Silvia and me the best middle-class life possible.

After what seemed like an idyllic childhood, I was ready to advance my studies. I entered in first place to the Toulouse-Lautrec institute to study graphic design—even when my father wanted me to be an architect—back in 1990. After that, I worked in advertising, multimedia, digital, and print companies non-stop, and won national and international awards. This was the career I dreamed of.

But when my mother died in 2006, I left my job of ten years at El Comercio newspaper to focus on my personal life. I met my husband in 2007, left my entire family, friends, culture and started my new life in the United States in 2009.

It was hard to start from zero in a new country, even if I was able to speak English. I did freelance projects before landing my first American job: bilingual sales associate at Victoria's Secret. I never thought I would be working at a mall. Resilience is part of my DNA, and I had to overcome the challenge of many professional immigrants who are well-prepared but don't have connections or prior jobs in the US.

After my fashion role, I was a freelancer for an advertising agency in Pennsylvania and a designer for a small print shop in Delaware.

In 2013, I joined Chase as a bilingual graphic designer to work on Spanish-English campaigns. After five years in the marketing services team, I joined Chase Pay managing campaigns for multinational clients. Soon I discovered Adelante, a business resource group that supports Latinos. I found my new *"familia!"* We learn together, share the difficulties to stand out in this competitive market, and the lack of representation of people of color.

Currently, I hold my dream role working at Chase Auto. I work with an amazing team to make magic happen. I was always a fan of sports cars and a firm believer of the law of attraction, so it was only matter of time until I got to work with Aston Martin iconic masterpieces.

My now ex-husband and I decided to go our separate ways during the COVID-19 pandemic. We are co-parenting a happy, artsy, and talented girl. She is studying in a bilingual charter school, because Spanish is important to us.

During the first inspection of my new house, I put my name and my daughter's name in one of the wood structures. It was the sign of a new beginning, and a bright future ahead.

Your story may be similar or totally different, but my advice is not to see challenges as obstacles. Look at them as an opportunity to learn and to test your ability and wit while having fun in the process!

BIOGRAPHY

Monica Sánchez Farfán is the marketing strategy manager for Aston Martin Financial Services at Chase Auto. She is an award-winning graphic designer with a Master of Arts degree. She was born in Peru and worked at the most important newspaper in Latin America, El Comercio.

Monica has been involved in activities oriented to inspire employees, including Hispanic Heritage Month events, mentoring young Latinos and Afro-Americans, as well as her Adelante leadership role at Chase in Delaware. She is an avid Zumba dancer, fashionista, has an artsy six-year-old daughter, and enjoys traveling the world while searching for delicious Peruvian food at each stop!

I CHASED HAPPINESS AND IT LED TO SUCCESS

CARLA SANTIAGO

"I may not be the smartest person in the room, but I can always be the most prepared."

We all know that success takes preparation, persistence, courage, dedication, and hard work, but where is the pursuit of happiness in the road to becoming successful? For me, chasing happiness was the added factor that led to my success.

I was raised in San Juan, Puerto Rico, by two working parents who taught me that education was the most important tool to be able to follow my dreams. When I was young, before my father dropped me off at school in the mornings, he would ask me to stand in front of the mirror, look at my reflection, and say, *"Yo puedo. Yo voy a mí."* This simple act instilled in me a belief that I could achieve anything and everything.

I was raised with discipline. I was raised with high expectations to do my best and to take accountability for my actions. But, above all, I was raised with love, happiness, and trust, by parents that never missed a birthday, a school event, or a chance to help with my homework. As I grew up, I realized my parents' upbringing had set me up for success, but I also understood that my parents didn't want me to be rich or powerful; they wanted me to be happy. And with that as my ultimate goal, I have made the personal and career decisions that today allow me to describe my life as a successful one because I am always standing, freely, where I want to be.

Chasing happiness takes guts. For me, sometimes that meant quitting prestigious, high-paying jobs or asking for a raise when I was being undervalued, going on a solo road trip through Portugal, and asking for forgiveness, even when it was difficult. In my pursuit of happiness, I have also been fired from the wrong job, recovered from bad relationships, and pushed my body to its limit to become a triathlete after a skiing accident that required knee surgery. Taking chances for your happiness does not always play out how you intend it to, but it can always lead to valuable lessons.

I have learned there are many ingredients to happiness, and the right mix is different for everyone. In my journey, this has been getting an education; becoming trilingual; developing emotional intelligence; traveling the world; treating everyone with generosity and respect; and knowing that my family is my unconditional safety, always there to encourage me to fly as high as I can and catch me if I fall. My mother always told me that happiness also requires humility, to know that I may not be the smartest person in the room, but I can always be the most prepared. And preparation can never be overestimated in giving you the self-confidence you need to fight for your dreams.

I know this story is supposed to be about me, but I want this story to be about you, because I want to see generations of successful and happy Latinos and Latinas everywhere. When you are chasing happiness, like I always am, you are on a constant journey to not only know yourself, but to also respect that self. Finding your passion, accepting your strengths and weaknesses, and understanding your self-worth will make you successful, no matter what.

BIOGRAPHY

Carla Santiago is the general manager of Edelman's Miami office, where she leads a multilingual, multicultural team of corporate, brand, international affairs, digital, and creative communicators. She is an energetic brand marketing and corporate communications executive, with an accomplished track record developing and implementing strategic communication plans for leading global consumer and hospitality brands in the US Hispanic and Latin America markets.

As a results-oriented leader with an established reputation for client relationship management and integrated teams collaboration, Carla offers strategic counsel across agency clients, and drives new business efforts across the Edelman network.

LEAVING A LEGACY SHE WILL BE PROUD OF!

MARIA DE LOURDES SAONA

"I woke up every morning with a drive to do better for my community. I didn't always know what that looked like, but I kept going."

Growing up Hispanic in the Bronx, during the seventies and eighties in New York City was AWESOME! The soundtrack of my young life was a compilation of Hector Lavoe, Lisa Lisa and Cult Jam, and Grand Master Flex—and the energy was thrilling. The streets of my neighborhood were filled with works of art much like Basquiat, with graffiti worthy of being in museums.

My parents immigrated from Ecuador in the seventies to make a better life for themselves, and found refuge in the South Bronx, NYC, circa 1971. My dad was a shipping clerk for a hat factory, and my mom was a seamstress for leather wholesalers. They both had the grit to withstand long hours of factory work, but not being able to speak the language forced them to navigate many barriers of discrimination.

My dad was a dedicated hard worker, devoted to his family, and humble to the core. My mom, through perseverance, became a successful business owner. My parents always advocated for my higher education since I was always a great student. Thankfully, I became the first in my family to graduate college, as I acquired a marketing and finance degree from the world-renowned New York University.

I since have gone on to work for Fortune 500 companies within their multicultural marketing divisions. I had a successful career in the Latin music industry, promoting the careers of many mega Latin artists like Marc Anthony, Ricky Martin, Selena, Shakira, and Vicente Fernandez, to name a few. I worked for American companies specifically targeting the Hispanic market, since I understood the demographic. It is truly fulfilling to use my expertise and knowledge to help companies recognize the value and worth Latinos have and will continue to have on this country.

But by being so focused on my career, I realized I didn't get around to forming my own family. However, at the age of forty-four, I was blessed to give birth to a beautiful baby girl I named Evita Marina. Evita's big brown eyes study my every move, which in turn inspires me to do good with every loving gesture, in every task, because I realize her brain is absorbing every bit of our life together. She is forever mine, and I am forever hers. I am bound by a love I have never known until now. In the most precious way, motherhood has changed me forever.

Today, I am committed to leaving Evita a legacy she can be proud of. In the past year as community outreach leader for *Hispanic Star*, I have been part of an amazing movement geared to help, elevate, and support our community. I can proudly say I was part of the solution when the recent global pandemic hit. I woke up every morning with a drive to do better for my community. I didn't always know what that looked like, but I kept going.

BIOGRAPHY

Maria de Lourdes Saona is an accomplished event marketing professional who started her career in the Latin music industry, then pivoted and entered the event marketing arena, where she worked for companies like Empire Blue Cross Blue Shield, Verizon, and Nissan USA.

She made a huge impact in the branding of these household names by increasing their market value. Maria currently works for Legends Digital, a boutique agency specializing in creating digital content for businesses in the United States.

In her free time, she enjoys volunteering, spending time with her three-year-old daughter, family, and friends, and cooking international dishes.

AGUSTINA SARTORI

"People believe in you and what your team built and, most excitingly, what you and your team can create. When that happens, for me, it's everything—it's the reason why I started."

As an engineer, I was passionate about creating technology that solved problems, and doing so in a space I experienced as a woman helped me identify the opportunity to think creatively. I was always more interested in technology than in beauty, but as an engineer, I saw the chance to create, build, and innovate, which opened a world of possibilities and led me to create GlamST, my augmented reality technology company based in Uruguay.

It was important for me to have a grounded mission for GlamST, so that everyone from employees to potential partners understood my vision. I always felt strongly about the direction of my company and visualized the path from Uruguay to Chile, and, while there, discovered that I was not that different from entrepreneurs in San Francisco.

I believed that if we wanted to grow, we needed to be in the

US, understand the market, and meet the right people; play in the first league, but always with our technology team in Uruguay. My determination helped me build on a vision I trusted and opened GlamST to brands like Ulta Beauty, which would later acquire us. Ulta Beauty believed in our diverse, international, high-skilled team and what we could create together from the beginning, giving us the opportunity to take everything we imagined to the next level.

Before the acquisition, my company served as Ulta Beauty's augmented reality (AR) partner. It was through this process I realized how essential it was to hold on to those who champion your mission and understand your vision. I was lucky to have one of my investors and a best friend that had sold his company a year prior mentor me through the process. It also made a big difference to have someone in the room I could relate to: Maria Salcedo, another Latina leading corporate development at the time. I look back and I think that, as Latinas, we helped build bridges within our teams to make a successful acquisition where our culture and values played an important role.

Throughout my career, I've fostered relationships that helped me continue to push forward on my journey. I believe that by leading with authenticity and trust, people believe in you and what your team built and, most excitingly, what you and your team can create. When that happens, for me, it's everything—it's the reason why I started.

BIOGRAPHY

Agustina Sartori is the founder and CEO at GlamST, an augmented reality (AR) technology company. Following GlamST's acquisition by Ulta Beauty in 2018, the biggest US beauty retailer, Agustina began serving as director of AR innovation. In this role, she works with the digital innovation team to develop AR experiences, AI, and machine learning.

Currently, a resident of San Francisco, she is originally from Uruguay, where she received her telematics engineering degree from University of Montevideo.

Agustina successfully raised more than $2 million from investors in Silicon Valley and globally she is an Endeavor entrepreneur, 500 Startups alumni, Plug&Play, ANII, and StartupChile; she has worked with world-class clients such as L'Oreal, EsteeLauder, Dufry, Clarins, and Neiman Marcus.

HOPE

STEVEN SEGARRA

"To me, to be Dominican means to endure in the face of adversity, represent the underrepresented, and stand up for those who are unable."

As a baseball player from the streets of the Dominican Republic, I felt inspired when I saw players like Big Papi, who also grew up on the streets, eventually become Major League Baseball superstars. In baseball, I saw an opportunity to overcome the socioeconomic barriers that prevent poor Latinxs from achieving their dreams.

When I was fourteen, I was hit in the eye with a baseball; that threatened not only my sight, but my dreams of becoming a professional athlete as well. I felt lost and hopeless. That hope was restored, however, through the intense compassion doctors demonstrated during my care, which motivated me to continue pursuing my dreams. The complex terms and intricate procedures performed on me sparked my curiosity and passion for medicine, and after extensive treatment, I was able to return to the field.

Unfortunately, my career was cut short when I suffered a back injury that cost me a full baseball scholarship to a Division 1 program. Having no idea what to do next, I was devastated.

Depression began to creep in when I slowly realized the injury would persist, and I was never going to play again. It grew difficult to get out of bed on some days, but I thought back to the hopeless moments after my eye injury, the way the doctors lifted my spirits, and how, if not for them, I would never have reached such a high level of play. I soon discovered that my purpose was to provide others with the same opportunity and hope that those physicians gave me at a young age.

My desire to serve led me to the underserved communities in the *bateyes* of the Dominican Republic. I still remember the little girl who played ever so joyfully with a cardboard box in the middle of the dirt street, and her father, a sugarcane harvester who developed cataracts after decades of long hours under the Caribbean sun. I was humbled as he explained his fear of no longer being able to support his family, but I reassured him that, with our help, he may regain his sight. Through this experience, I gained a profound new perspective on the role of the physician.

The physician, a source of knowledge and wisdom, must also take on the burden of easing the soul and calming the restless spirit. I am reminded of a line from the Dominican National Anthem, which says, *"Mas quisqueya la indómita y brava, siempre altiva la frente alzará."*

To me, to be Dominican means to endure in the face of adversity, represent the underrepresented, and stand up for those who are unable. This resilience is what resides within the modern physician and serves as the hope they must impart upon their patients. Through these experiences, I have learned to use my goals and ambitions as a medium to ignite the same passion in others, so that I may not only heal the bodies of my patients but restore their spirit and provide them with hope as well.

BIOGRAPHY

Steven Segarra is a first-generation immigrant and college student from the Dominican Republic. He has a BS in biochemistry and is earning his medical degree at Temple University. Steven has published neuroscience research in prestigious scientific journals such as *Nature and Nature Neuroscience*. Throughout the COVID-19 pandemic, Steven used his passion for technology to bring people together virtually via livestreaming. He plans on using his platform to educate and garner interest in medicine moving forward. Connect with Steven on Twitch at twitch.tv/thboywndr and on social media @thboywndr!

A PACT TO LIVE

OLGA LUISA SERRANO-ROSARIO

"Living with a purpose is the way."

My story starts with one word, POSITIVE. Imagine this: the professional and life plans are on track. You lead a manufacturing plant, the first woman in your company in Puerto Rico. You are young, you love, you are loved, and have a life. You read a piece of paper that's handed to you. It reads: positive, breast cancer. What to do?

Well, I cried, shouted out, doubted. I felt anger, fear, sadness, disappointment, pain, and despair. I let every emotion have its way out. I mean, one needs to let them out to have space to welcome and work on the recovery. I had two blasts, one of the side effects of the chemotherapy and radiation, the other of joy because of the support and love of my mom, dad, sister, niece, and friends. I remember with joy the "chemo parties" that my family used to throw.

Even when I spent the whole day in bed feeling sick, these

parties filled me with energy, encouragement, and love. Yes, I overcame cancer! Now, what do I do?

After that experience, my life perspective changed: "living with a purpose is the way." So, I moved from engineering and leading a manufacturing site to human resources and joined the American Cancer Society to spend quality time with my loved ones and to give back by educating others about cancer. This change in mindset allowed me to dedicate myself to service, both at work and life.

On a "normal" day, I check in with my team to plan the week, work with my global team on development solutions for employees, facilitate training or workshop sessions, and work. There are two things I enjoy the most about the job: the opportunity to coach an employee on their development and career path, by being able to help them discover what they want to be and see them succeed; and to work on the Employee Resources Groups (ERG), where the action focuses on addressing inequity issues, tolerance, and acceptance. To me, the goal is beyond a percentage of representation. It is about creating an environment where everyone has equal opportunity to be in the game. ERGs can be the vehicles to advance equity strategy and social justice.

To every person reading this, I humbly recommend having a purpose in life. Discover your passion and dare to make it more important that money and power. Pursue your talent and be courageous to express it. Use your voice! Act now. Don't wait for a threat to happen to make changes. Start living your life to the fullest now, pay attention to your body and health, help others, and stop caring what others think about that career switch. Life is much more than just success and work achievements. I am unaware of how my story will be in the future or how it will end. I do know that now it is the way it started, with the word POSITIVE.

BIOGRAPHY

Olga Luisa Serrano-Rosario was born and raised in Puerto Rico, where she has lived all her life. A Caribbean woman that uses the pronouns she/her/hers, Olga earned a Bachelor's degree in Industrial Engineering from the University of Puerto Rico and got a Master's degree in Engineering Management from the Polytechnic University of Puerto Rico. Olga has been working for Medtronic PLC for thirty years, about sixteen years as engineer and leader of manufacturing operations, and fourteen in the human resources arena. The last five she has spent as leader of learning and development for global manufacturing.

In her free time, Olga enjoys being with her family, super-sprinting triathlons, ziplining, and skydiving.

MAKING PEOPLE DEVELOPMENT A TOP PRIORITY

MARCO SERRATO

"We need to break the paradigm of a three-stage life: you study, you work, you retire. That is not the present, and even less the future of moving forward."

Not long ago, the competitive advantage among individuals, organizations, and different regions worldwide belonged to those who "knew the most"—a knowledge economy. Now it accrues to those who know how to learn the most—a learning economy. The emerging needs and trends that took place under the COVID-19 pandemic illustrated this through new skills and capabilities that we all had to learn and develop in a short time frame. And for better or worse, this trend will continue to take place as new technologies, challenges, and societal changes will continue to arise in this world we all live in.

Just think of a young person entering university this year, who will probably be at the peak of his or her career in around 2050, under a certainly different world. So, creating a transformational evolution of higher education to be relevant under such context requires developing novel services for adults learning while working—which is precisely what we have developed at the University of Chicago through professional development programs that have reached individuals in more than thirty countries all over the world in the last two years.

Spanish novelist Miguel de Cervantes said, "The man who is prepared has his battle half fought." Prior to the COVID-19 pandemic, we acknowledged the fact that education is moving from a straight line (learning first in school and then applying that same learning throughout one's tenure at work) to a continuum of lifelong learning—learning and applying learning in several cycles of continuous personal evolution throughout our lives. To support this, I was honored to collaborate with great instructors, faculty, and staff at the University of Chicago to develop a pipeline of professional development programs offered under online and digital formats, using innovative learning technologies and pedagogy. This portfolio of programs has supported adults all over the world to develop the skills and knowledge they all require nowadays.

One key takeaway that I usually hear from these professionals and the organizations they work for is that "the world we are in right now is challenging." So, in order to face it in a successful manner, we need to break the paradigm of a three-stage life: you study, you work, you retire. We need to be learning in a continuous manner throughout our lives and to make people's development a top priority. We are, in short, being asked by our challenging times to be nothing less than exceptional.

No one can predict our future exactly, but we can be confident about two things: it is going to be different, and it must be rooted in today's world. To succeed in it, we have to think and act in ways we have never thought before, especially if we want ourselves, our organizations, and our society to go to places they have never been before.

BIOGRAPHY

Marco Serrato serves as associate provost at the University of Chicago, where he leads the expansion of professional development programs for executive and other continuing education students.

Marco has a global understanding of professional education. He has developed training initiatives in more than thirty countries worldwide and is an emeritus board member of the International Consortium for University-Based Executive Education (UNICON). His contributions have been featured by international media including the World Economic Forum and the United Nations, among others.

Marco holds a double-degree PhD in Industrial Engineering from Iowa State University and from Tecnológico de Monterrey.

CREATE WHAT YOU WANT TO SEE

DR. MERARY SIMEON

"Knowing that giving up was not an option, racism, cultural norms, doubt, fear, and the countless failures I experienced could not stop me from becoming the wife, mother, daughter, sister, friend, and leader I am today."

"Nadie se parece a mí." No one looks like me. Anxiety, fear, and hopelessness filled my heart and mind as I struggled to find my place in the world. I was born in San German, Puerto Rico, to two hard-working parents who embarked into the unknown to create opportunities for their children. It was around midnight when we arrived for the first time at Newark Airport. It was a cold night, and I saw traces of snow on the ground. The cold made my bones ache, but it did not stop me from moving forward. I did not realize that cold, dark, and dreary night would represent what was to come.

My parents worked hard, faced many challenges, and sacrificed for our family. My parents taught me something education could not teach me. They taught me that the same power that rose Jesus from the dead lives in me, and through Him, I can do all things.

They planted the seed of possibility and watered it with faith, resilience, and persistence. For me, giving up is not an option, and creating what I want to see is my mission.

Learning a new language was difficult, but nothing could be more challenging than growing up without leaders that did not look like me. The only Latina leaders existed in the *novelas,* and most times, the villain was a beautiful woman with status and power. A power she abused for self-interest while destroying the dreams and confidence of those around her.

Growing up, I was not privileged to learn from Latina leaders. However, my parents planted the seeds that became the most powerful tools I needed to create what I wanted to see. Through the mentorship of a woman of color, I turned my life around and decided to become everything I wanted to see.

To create what I wanted to see, I began to envision the possibilities. Imagination is powerful; while I could not see successful Latinas in the position of power, I began to imagine myself holding a high school diploma, graduating college, working in an office, buying my parents a home, being an author, an inspirational speaker, and a leader in a position to make a difference. Knowing that giving up was not an option, racism, cultural norms, doubt, fear, and the countless failures I experienced could not stop me from becoming the wife, mother, daughter, sister, friend, and leader I am today.

The key to my success is discipline through H.E.R.A.C.T. It stands for healing, elevating my mindset, and respecting myself to achieve what I want to see while renewing my confidence to sustain transformation.

I have learned to take intentional actions towards what I want to see. Some days, I fail miserably, while other days, I breathe victory, but the vision remains the same: I create what I want to see. Do not let the world limit what you can achieve. Seeds of greatness are inside you. It is time to shine.

BIOGRAPHY

Dr. Merary Simeon is a proven and celebrated human resources executive who is community-minded and people-invested. She is a working mother, co-founder of the What Rules!? Podcast, a book author, board member, and kingdom work advocate.

Dr. Simeon's diverse experiences have equipped her with a deep understanding of the needs and opportunities critical to leaders at all levels. Dr. Simeon holds a Doctorate in Strategic Leadership and a Master's degree in Human Resources. She is a native of Puerto Rico and resides in Frisco, Texas, with her family. She credits her success to Jesus Christ, Philippians 4:13.

ELDA STANCO DOWNEY

"Ocupa tu lugar, my mother said, and that is how I carved my rightful place in the world."

When my father left war-torn Italy as a stowaway on a grain cargo ship at the age of fifteen, he did not head to the United States, where his father had been born. Rather, he headed to Venezuela, a young, booming land of opportunity. At that same time, my mother, who had just turned twenty-one, was a teacher, with plans to pursue a PhD in pharmacology. The two eventually met on an airplane—one, an entrepreneurial, self-made businessman who had not finished the third grade, the other, la Doctora Rojas, the head of quality at a transnational pharmaceutical laboratory.

Six decades later, here I am—a PhD, like my Venezuelan mami, turned entrepreneurial business owner, like my Italian papi. And now, a US citizen, like my Italian great-grandparents were decades ago.

My family history is one of journeys, of travels, of voyages, of adventures into uncharted territories. It has been reflected in my own *wanderlust,* in my thirst for new lands, new peoples. But in this nomadic quest there are inevitable moments of doubt and identity crises—I feel like this place is home, but everyone around me clearly signals to me that I do not belong. That I do not belong. That my hair is too dark or too curly, or too much of both of these things. That my accent is too different. That I am a just a girl with an Ivy League education, just a girl. That I am too loud. That my lipstick is too red. That I am too outspoken and too hard-willed, and women are not supposed to be like that. That I am exotic. Where are you from, exactly, Elda? And how does this not slowly, over years and across places and spaces, not start to slowly nudge at your identity, at your core configuration of who you are?

"Ocupa tu lugar," my mother said, and that is how I carved my rightful place in the world. I am Doctor Stanco Downey, my mother's daughter, *la hija of la Doctora* Rojas. This is my scholarly side; this is the professor who teaches medical Spanish to aspiring MDs and literature to passionate readers; the author of articles and the presenter at conference panels. I am my father's daughter too; this is my builder and creator side, this is the ideas, the new ways of doing business. This is the ever-optimistic individual, the one who easily wins and dusts off my pants when I am not that fortunate.

As a resident and now citizen of the United States, I have embraced and now own the Hispanic, Latino/a, Latinx monikers we all receive. And what I have learned from my *mami's ocupa tu lugar* is that I am any and all of these identities—but it is I who define what these words mean. Not those who utilize them to categorize them to put our people down or to stereotype us. It is we who must own these and master them to then make wherever we go, home.

BIOGRAPHY

Elda Stanco Downey is founder and CEO of Roanoke Spanish, a cultural intelligence firm, and is on the faculty of the Virginia Tech Carilion School of Medicine. Born in Venezuela, she grew up trilingual, speaking Spanish and Italian at home and English at her international school.

Elda is passionate about community advocacy, serving on numerous nonprofit boards and by appointment from City Council and the Governor of Virginia. She earned an honors Bachelor's degree in Psychology and Romance Languages & Literatures at The University of Chicago. She holds an MA and a PhD in Hispanic Studies from Brown University.

THE "AMERICAN DREAM"

ALAN TORRES

"DACA doesn't grant me any right or privilege over any American citizen; rather, it gives me my own opportunity to rise as an active member of society."

To me, DACA embodies the "American Dream"—the opportunity for a validated history, a stable present, and a better future. DACA doesn't grant me any right or privilege over any American citizen; rather, it gives me my own opportunity to rise as an active member of society.

But let me be clear: I sought ways to pursue this path on my own, even without any assistance. I earned my college degree and paid for it out of pocket, before DACA was a thing. Imagine this: I pursued education without even having the assurance that I could apply it to any career or benefit from it in any way. Truly, it was a leap of faith.

They say that success is when opportunity meets preparation, and DACA was just that, an opportunity. It was an opportunity to bring my skillset into the market and make a better life for myself and my family. Isn't that the true definition of the "American Dream?" With DACA, my dreams were no longer restricted, just because of my place of birth. And I was now being measured purely by my abilities and skillset.

Where would I be without DACA? Honestly, I don't know, but I am reminded of the frugality of it all every eighteen months, when the time comes to renew my permit, and anxiety kicks in as I wait for the DACA renewal to be approved before I am forced to take a leave of absence at work. I am reminded every time politicians argue over the legality and ethical dilemma of it. I, and many like me, continue to live in a nebulous area of the law—with an expiration date stamped on our backs. And even so, I am still grateful for the opportunity. But I yearn for a more permanent stability.

The first time my permit was approved, I remember the freedom and peace of mind I felt, as I was able to drive a car without fear of being deported due to a traffic stop, for the first time ever. I remember the first time I saw a cop and didn't feel fear. I remember being able to open a bank account and seeing my name printed on a bank card, for the first time ever. It felt like coming up for a breath of air after drowning in a sea. Simply, it was life changing—for the first time ever, I had the opportunity to be celebrated for my accomplishments instead of being tolerated for my limitations.

This is what I know for sure: Without DACA, my life would be very different. DACA allows me, and an entire generation, to escape a vicious cycle of working lower-wage jobs, getting paid under the table, living without the possibility of buying a house. I would have never been able to become an engineer, to become an IBMer, to become a leader in my company. More importantly, without these opportunities, I would have been confined to a different world restricting me, my wife, and children to a life of limited opportunities and possibilities. Without DACA, the "American Dream" is shattered—my talent would have been wasted, and I would have never been allowed to live a life fulfilling my potential.

BIOGRAPHY

Alan Torres is a "Dreamer"—a person brought to the US as a child and whose legal status remains in limbo. Alan joined IBM in 2016 as a software engineer for Watson Health. He has transitioned from engineering to sales and is currently on assignment as chief of staff for the general manager of consumer, retail, and travel industries.

Alan has advocated before Congress and the US Senate on immigration reform legislation. In 2018, he was hand-selected to address IBM's most senior world executives discussing his advocacy work, world views, and relevant topics in which he received a standing ovation.

ADRIENNE VALENCIA GARCIA

"An education is something no one can ever take away from you."

Growing up in a predominantly white neighborhood, I often found myself exhausted from living two different lives: there was my home life, where I spoke Spanish, we had big family parties with lots of salsa dancing and I spent my summers in Colombia with my grandparents; and my outside life, where I spoke English without an accent (not even a New York one!), often found myself defending Colombians from negative stereotypes, and sometimes even pretended not to be Hispanic at all.

My parents never let their differences deter them from their number-one priority. Like many immigrant families, their primary focus was making a better life for their children. In fact, one of their mantras was: "An education is something no one can ever take away from you." So, I always excelled in school and planned to be a professional, because that was the expectation. Not to mention that my parents were never impressed with a grade below 100, even if I had the highest grade! The response would be, "But it's not 100."

Truth be told, they were extremely proud. That was just their way of keeping me on my toes—and thankfully, it worked. They also showed me the importance of a hard work ethic and dedication to excellence. My dad took night classes to become a field service engineer, fixing medical equipment like MRIs and CAT-Scan machines. My mom worked a variety of roles at American Express, until they moved her department out of state, but she was undeterred and decided to get her beautician's license, so she could set her own hours as an in-home stylist. Way ahead of her time!

Being first-generation meant my parents were not familiar with a lot of the school-related decisions and processes I needed to navigate to secure the education they dreamed of for me. Whether it was finding the best high school and going through the application process, to registering for and studying for the SATs, or even deciding where to go to college and what courses I should take, I was on my own. That is when I learned the power of networking, even though I did not learn the term until much later in life. I was always curious, asked lots of questions, and sought to learn from others.

I can say without a doubt that I would not be where I am today without actively curating—and maintaining—my community of mentors and leaders who I relied upon for guidance along the way. That is why I am such a passionate mentor, resource, and advocate for others, particularly young women and people of color. I genuinely feel joy each time someone shares that my advice helped them succeed in some way, whether getting a new role or a raise.

We are stronger together, and whenever I can pull someone up or amplify them in a room they do not have access to yet, I am there for it!

BIOGRAPHY

Adrienne Valencia Garcia is the proud daughter of Colombian immigrants who came to the US in the sixties, landing in New York. She has experienced many firsts, from being the first in her family born in the US, to being the first in her family to earn a four-year college degree, the first attorney in her family, and the first executive, having been promoted to the executive ranks of IBM's law department in 2018.

Adrienne is currently the general counsel for the Cognitive Systems business and continues supporting blockchain transactions. She is a passionate advocate for diversity, equity, and inclusion, actively serving in the leadership council for Legal Diversity and the Hispanic National Bar Association, as well as mentoring a number of rising Hispanic talent.

NELI VAZQUEZ ROWLAND

"When you pay attention to the trends, anything is possible."

When I first entered the financial world, I never imagined that later I would be able to use what I had learned to become an advocate for those impacted by poverty and homelessness. Still, somewhere along the way, that is precisely what happened. Studying financial trends, I learned to slow down, pay attention, and listen to what the social landscape was telling me. All these things would prove beneficial later.

Years ago, in our Chicago neighborhood, A Safe Haven was born out of a desire to do more and give back as a result of understanding what the facts were telling us. Feeling financially stable and ready to make a difference, my husband Brian and I decided to do something that would positively impact our community by purchasing an apartment property near the Logan Square area. This would not be just any property investment; we had something special in mind for the building.

At this point, I had learned that research was the key to

making informed decisions. I realized that the best opportunities had come when I kept my eyes and ears open for data and trends. Ultimately, this research method helped us turn the thirteen-unit apartment complex property into a home for those suffering from substance abuse and addiction. We had a vision for this project that was based on what the research was telling us. Rehabilitation facilities weren't always working, and the price often too high for those that needed them most.

In the early years, we would spend our time and money rehabbing the property, furnishing the apartments, and adding landscaping to make the property feel like home to all those who would come to call the property theirs. While we initially intended to sell the property, after some time, we realized that our hard work was starting to pay off.

We then found ourselves asking how we could do more. In an effort to help our residents get back on their feet, we realized that employment was the next step. To tackle this need, we trained and hired some of the people we served, including acquiring a landscaping company, and then we started hiring landscapers for our social enterprise business. We have since had the opportunity to expand job placements to several different careers, working to find positions that our residents will succeed in—and helping them find financial independence. Over the last twenty-six years, we have reached 130 thousand people, offering them a place to stay and opportunities that impact the trajectory of their lives.

A Safe Haven has helped us reach the lives of those who need help the most. While we have touched our own community with this project, we feel our job is not yet done. At A Safe Haven, we continue to invest in at-risk communities and create programs and initiatives that contribute to giving back in our community and across the country.

For me, founding A Safe Haven was proof that when you pay attention to the trends, have a passion for helping and empowering the lives of those in need, and have lots of faith, anything is possible. In fact, you might just find your next opportunity ready to present itself when you start with the research.

BIOGRAPHY

Chicago-born Neli Vazquez Rowland is a passionate advocate for the homeless. In 1994, Neli and her husband Brian launched A Safe Haven (ASH) to address the root causes of the growing opioid and homeless epidemics. ASH is lauded as one of the most successful, vertically integrated delivery systems and continuum of care models providing transitional housing and individualized social services. ASH has helped 130 thousand people transform their lives to independence and self-sufficiency.

She is a sought-after speaker, a co-author of landmark state legislation, and creator of Chicago's first medical COVID-19 respite center serving vulnerable populations. She is the author of *HEALING*, an anthology of success stories told by A Safe Haven alumni.

NOTHING IS TOO FAR

DR. AUGUSTO VEGA

"Thirty years later, today I know that nothing is too far—you just need a plan and enough love to execute it properly!"

I fell in love with computers very early in my life, as a kid in Realicó, a rural town in Argentina. Without internet and living in an isolated area, getting information about leading edge developments was difficult; still, I tried to read every possible book or magazine that passed through my hands. At the same time, I also learned that the real advances in the area were taking place "somewhere else," very far—too far!—away from my hometown. It could have been easy to give up and to put my dreams aside. But I did not.

I created a plan, one that could take me all the way to reach my dream: become a computer scientist for a world-renowned organization. My modest-yet-ambitious plan was based in two premises: cross one bridge at a time and work hard.

I moved to Buenos Aires, Argentina's capital city, to pursue my computer engineering degree. Was this easy? Not at all! Suddenly, I found myself living alone in a huge city, far from my family and friends, out of my safe place. I tried to keep my mind clear towards a successful graduation to execute the next step in the plan: a PhD program abroad!

I then moved to Spain to start my doctoral program in the computer architecture field at the Polytechnic University of Catalonia. What a journey! Again, I had to start over a "new life" in a new place, this time seven thousand miles apart from my family. I felt guilty: yes, in some ways, I was leaving my family behind. But they supported me, because they believed in me, and they trusted my plan. "Go and chase your dreams. It's time for you to fly, and to fly high! We'll always be here," they told me. But they weren't "always there." My father passed away a few years later; so did my grandparents. (I miss them every single day.) But moving back to Argentina was not going to change things, so I kept moving forward.

A couple of years into my PhD degree, an opportunity to join IBM Research came up. I didn't think twice and immediately accepted it! This is how I joined the IBM T. J. Watson Research Center in 2010, where I met some of the most influential people of my life, including Dr. Pradip Bose. Through them, I discovered the happiness side of doing research. Through them, I finally became a researcher.

Thirty years later, I'm proud of what I've achieved and happy with my life. Today I know that nothing is too far—you just need a plan and enough love to execute it properly!

Finally, there is one special person around who this journey revolves. Her name is Chiara, and she is my wife. Her support has been my source of strength and I hope I have made sense to her life too. With countless difficulties along the path, I couldn't be happier to have traveled it along with her.

BIOGRAPHY

Dr. Augusto Vega is a senior research staff member at the IBM T. J. Watson Research Center, involved in work in the areas of heterogeneous systems and edge AI computing. He made contributions to the field with top-tier publications and has been appointed as General Chair of the 2024 International Symposium on Computer Architecture (ISCA), the flagship conference in computer architecture. Dr. Vega has more than twenty issued US patents, several peer-reviewed publications, and a co-guest edited book. At IBM, Dr. Vega helped spawn off the new area of cloud-backed, swarm-AI edge cognition systems. He is the CTO of the DARPA-funded EPOCHS project, and a member of the Mayflower Autonomous Ship (MAS) project.

FROM THE FARM TO THE FOREFRONT OF TECH

JESUS VIDAURRI

"We all have the ability to come from nothing and become something."

It was 3:30 a.m., and my alarm had just gone off. As I began to drag myself out of bed, I could hear my mom scrambling in the kitchen preparing lunch for my dad and me. At the same time, I could hear my father turn the truck on so it could warm up, as it was one of the coldest weeks in Florida in a long time. I put on my long sleeve shirt, my denim jeans, and a pair of work boots, and I started to head out the door. My mom quickly stopped me and said, "Mijo! Don't forget your sun hat (in Spanish of course)." My dad and I finally left the house and made it to the work bus in time to head to the fields by 6 a.m.

This was a typical winter and summer break for me in high school. Waking up at the crack of dawn to head to the tomato fields with my father and uncle to learn what it was truly like to earn a dollar in the United States. It was a lesson that I never forgot, and to this day I use as fuel to motivate me.

This was a similar scenario for a lot of folks in my town. I grew up in a small immigrant community in Southwest Florida called Immokalee, the epicenter for the world's tomatoes and other produce. It's a town known for its football stars as well as its demographic makeup of predominantly Mexican, Haitian, and Guatemalan immigrants.

Growing up, I didn't have much, but I always appreciated the little I did have. It was this same appreciation that motivated me to make it to college as a first-generation student and eventually find myself a career in technology so many years later. I still remember one of my first interviews that got me into tech recruiting. The question was "What are you hoping to get out of this job," and my response, "The ability to work in A/C." I don't know why I said that; perhaps it was my father's words from when we were under the blazing hot sun in the middle of the tomato fields.

Today, I strive to be an expert in my field. I came into tech not knowing a single thing about it. Over time, I challenged myself to learn more and become a resource to those seeking opportunities in technology. It wasn't until I found myself at my current company, that my true calling came to fruition, and that was to bring diversity, equity, and inclusion to the technology space. I've learned from some of the best diversity practitioners in the industry and am comfortable enough to be my authentic self and share my story. This is what I felt set me apart from my peers. David Goggins, retired Navy Seal and Ultra Marathon runner, once said, "We all have the ability to come from nothing and become something," and this has resonated with me ever since!

BIOGRAPHY

A recruiter by practice and technologist at heart, Jesus Vidaurri currently supports Tech Data Corp. as their senior technical recruiter. He has worked in recruitment and staffing within the Tampa Bay area for over six years, all within the realm of technology, supporting roles from software development and cybersecurity to machine learning and data analytics.

Jesus obtained his bachelor's degree from the University of South Florida. He currently serves as the president for Blacks in Technology Tampa Chapter, as well as a member of the Young Professionals Board for Embarc Collective.

THE MEXICAN KID THAT NEVER LEARNED THE WORD IMPOSSIBLE

OSCAR ZEPEDA

"MEX I CAN."

Have you ever been told "Don't do it, it's not realistic," or "Don't do it, it's impossible, only these types of people can do it"? My life has always been like that, but I hope while reading my story, you can see that the more you work and the more you accomplish, those people that doubted you and told you that you couldn't will end up asking you how you did it.

For me, it all started in Guadalajara, Jalisco, Mexico. Raised by a single dad, I was the first case of a male parent in Jalisco to earn his kid's custody. He helped me be who I am, always telling me to become someone special.

In 2013, I came to the United States after I won an athletic scholarship to play soccer at Merrimack College. I arrived without visiting the college before, without being in Boston before, and without knowing anyone. I will always remember arriving at soccer practice with my roommate at the time (also Mexican) as the first two Mexicans ever to be in the college's team and hearing, "I am glad the Mexicans arrived for someone to cut the grass."

Despite the adversity and struggles of being in another country and having to pay for college without student loans, I managed to become the captain of the soccer team, the founder and president of the first-ever Latino student association at Merrimack, and finished with a summa cum laude honorary degree—and all while having four jobs that helped pay for my college career. There was always this image on my phone that said "Mexican" but for me, it always said, "MEX I CAN" and acted as a reminder.

In my senior year, I founded a company with my dad, OMZE Group, with two objectives: to promote, import, and distribute Mexican and Latino products in Massachusetts, mainly Tequila, and to consult and help small and medium Mexican and New England-based companies to grow and internationalize their businesses.

To get the alcohol wholesaler and importer alcohol licenses, it took me multiple workshops and self-teaching while in college in a process that took nearly two years. We did it because we were tired of hearing: "Mexican producers are not professional enough" and "they do not know how to sell internationally."

We have been able to help companies from Mexico to get their exportation requirements ready for their quality products to be exported from Mexico to the United States through OMZE's consulting mechanism. In 2019, we became the official business representative by the Jalisco state government for the New England Area, in which we connect small and medium businesses from Mexico with buyers and wholesalers in New England. Now, every year we organize commercial missions for Mexican companies to come to Boston and visit local buyers and distributors.

In early 2019, we released our tequila brand: Real Zepeda. Since our brand launched, we have developed relationships with restaurant and retailer owners and community leaders to embrace and empower Latino heritage and traditions in Massachusetts. So far, we have sold over four thousand cases, which translates into almost $800 thousand in revenue, and more than one hundred jobs in Mexico.

With my tequila business, I have been able to represent, educate, and show Massachusetts the authenticity and traditions of Mexican and Latino people, while at the same time creating a direct connection with the producers and the hard-working immigrant communities. Finally, I became part of the youth programs held by Boston's Latinx Cultural Center, where I founded the summer program for youth entrepreneurs in the cultural center. In 2019, I was honored by *El Mundo* as one of the most influential Latinos 30 under 30.

BIOGRAPHY

Oscar Zepeda is originally from Guadalajara, Mexico. Zepeda graduated with a double major in international business and marketing and a minor in economics and earned his Master's degree in Applied Economics from Boston College.

While at Merrimack, Zepeda co-founded OMZE Group, an international consulting company, which seeks to aid small and medium-sized Latino businesses in achieving their international market objectives.

Today, Zepeda serves as the company's vice president, selected as one of the most influential young Latinos in *El Mundo's* Boston Latino 30 under 30. He has also since co-founded Real Zepeda Tequila, distributing it throughout Massachusetts and New England.

ABOUT THE AUTHOR

Claudia Romo Edelman is a social entrepreneur, an inspiring data-driven speaker, and a determined catalyst for positive change. As a recognized speaker, media contributor and advocate, Claudia is a leader for diversity, inclusion and equity, focused on unifying the U.S. Hispanic community, and promoting sustainability and purpose-driven activities, particularly within brands, tech, and the creative industries.

With an extraordinary background with global organizations, including the United Nations, UNICEF, and the World Economic Forum, she has collaborated and worked on humanitarian causes for 25 years with organizations such as (RED), the United Nations High Commissioner for Refugees (UNHCR), and the Global Fund to fight AIDS, tuberculosis, and malaria.

Claudia is Founder of the We Are All Human Foundation, a New York-based nonprofit foundation, dedicated to advancing the agenda of diversity, inclusion and equity through developing and hosting regional and local events, conducting research and developing research pieces/publications, creating content, and corporate activation.

She enjoys sports, traveling with her husband and two children, and speaks six languages.

ABOUT THE PUBLISHER

Jacqueline Camacho-Ruiz is a visionary social entrepreneur that has created an enterprise of inspiration. With 20 years of experience in the marketing and Public Relations industry, she has created two successful award-winning companies, established two nonprofit organizations, published 26 books, created a number of products, and held dozens of events around the world. She has received over 30 awards for her business acumen.

Jacqueline is currently the CEO of JJR Marketing, one of the fastest-growing top marketing and public relations agencies in Chicago, and Fig Factor Media, a media publishing company that helps individuals bring their books to life. Jacqueline is also the Founder of The Fig Factor Foundation, a not-for-profit organization dedicated to giving vision, direction, and structure to young Latinas as well as the President of Instituto Desarrollo Amazing Aguascalientes, the first youth center in Calvillo, Aguascalientes, Mexico, offering various hands-on experience, courses, and global connections to support international youth in defining their dreams.

Jacqueline currently serves as a board member for the World Leaders Forum, The Fig Factor Foundation, and the Alumni Executive Board at the College of DuPage. She is a recent graduate of the Stanford University Latino Business Action Network, and the Women Entrepreneurship Cohort 3 from DePaul University among others. Jacqueline is one of the few sports Latina airplane pilots in the United States.